Grammar Activities 1

Intermediate

Will Forsyth
Sue Lavender

PHOTOCOPIABLE

Macmillan Education

A division of Macmillan Publishers Limited

Companies and representatives throughout the world

ISBN 0 435 25094 9

© Will Forsyth, Sue Lavender 1994
Design and Illustration © Macmillan Publishers Limited 1998
Heinemann is a registered trademark of Reed Educational & Professional Publishing Limited

First published 1994

For John Lavender, to remember you always

Permission to copy

The material in this book is copyright. However, the publisher grants permission for copies of pages to be made without fee on those pages maked with the PHOTOCOPIABLE symbol.

Private purchasers may make copies for their own use or for use by classes of which they are in charge; school purchasers may make copies for use within and by the staff and students of the school only. This permission does not extend to additional schools or branches of an institution, who should purchase a separate master copy of the book for their own use.

For copying in any other circumstances, prior permission in writing must be obtained from the Publishers.

Designed by Helen Hible

Cover design by Stafford & Stafford

Illustrated by: Belinda Evans, Frank James, Satoshi Kambayashi, Mike Mosedale, Shaun Williams

Printed in Thailand

2008 2007 2006 2005 2004
17 16 15 14 13 12 11 10

Contents

1. Notes to the teacher
2. Adjectives with -ed and -ing 1
3. Adjectives with -ed and -ing 2
4. Adverbs of time   *since, for, ago*
5. Articles 1   use of *a* and *the*
6. Articles 2   use of *a* and *the*
7. Articles 3   *the* and zero article
8. Comparing 1   comparatives with *-er* and *more*
9. Comparing 2   comparatives with *-er* and *more*
10. Comparing 3   *as ... as*
11. Comparing 4   *as ... as*
12. Conditionals 1   first and second conditional
13. Conditionals 2   first and second conditional
14. Conjunctions 1   *in case, if, when, unless, as long as*
15. Conjunctions 2   *in case, if, when, unless, as long as*
16. Countable and uncountable 1   countability
17. Countable and uncountable 2   *money, people, work*, etc.
18. Countable and uncountable 3   *is, are, a, much* and *many*
19. Countable and uncountable 4   *is, are, a, much* and *many*
20. Countable and uncountable 5   frequently confused words
21. Futures 1   *will* and *going to*
22. Futures 2   *will* and *going to*
23. Futures 3   *will, going to* and present continuous
24. Futures 4   *will, going to* and present continuous
25. Futures 5   future simple and continuous
26. Futures 6   future simple and continuous
27. Futures 7   *will/shall*, present continuous, *going to*, future continuous
28. Have something done 1
29. Have something done 2
30. Indirect questions
31. Infinitive and gerund 1   infinitive of purpose
32. Infinitive and gerund 2   infinitive of purpose
33. Infinitive and gerund 3   verbs taking either infinitive or gerund
34. Modal verbs 1   *can, should, must*
35. Modal verbs 2   *can, should, must*
36. Modal verbs 3   *must* and *have to*
37. Modal verbs 4   *must* and *have to*
38. Passives 1   common signs
39. Passives 2   present and past simple, present perfect and modals
40. Passives 3   present and past simple, present perfect and modals
41. Passives 4   passive with *should*
42. Past and future
43. Past and present   questions
44. Past perfect and past simple 1

45	Past perfect and past simple 2	
46	Prepositions	prepositions after certain words
47	Present perfect	
48	Present perfect and past simple 1	
49	Present perfect and past simple 2	
50	Present perfect and past simple 3	
51	Present perfect and past simple 4	
52	Present perfect and past simple 5	
53	Present perfect simple and continuous 1	
54	Present perfect simple and continuous 2	
55	Present simple and continuous 1	
56	Present simple and continuous 2	
57	Present simple and continuous 3	stative and dynamic
58	Relative clauses 1	defining relative clauses
59	Relative clauses 2	defining relative clauses
60	Relative clauses 3	defining relative clauses
61	Relative clauses 4	defining relative clauses
62	Reporting 1	past perfect after *I realised, I discovered,* etc.
63	Reporting 2	tense changes
64	Reporting 3	tense changes
65	Reporting 4	tense changes
66	Substitution words and others	proforms, particles, etc.
67	Suggestions 1 *How about -ing? Let's ... Why don't we ...?* etc.	
68	Suggestions 2 *How about -ing? Let's ... Why don't we ...?* etc.	
69	Time phrases present simple after *if, unless,* etc.	
70	Too and enough 1	
71	Too and enough 2	
72	Used to	
73	Want someone to do something	
74	Wish 1	past simple
75	Wish 2	past perfect and past simple
76	Wish 3	past perfect and past simple
77	Word order	position of direct object and adverbs, e.g. *very much*
Review 1		
Review 2		
Review 3		
Review 4		
Review 5		
Answer key	Page 83	
Index	Page 91	
Questionnaire	Page 92	

Notes to the teacher

Grammar Activities 1 is for students at a mid-intermediate level including those just beginning a course for the Cambridge First Certificate examination. It is intended as a coursebook supplement. It provides presentation and consolidation, using a variety of contexts and approaches, of grammatical areas which cause learners problems at this level. It contains 76 free-standing worksheets arranged alphabetically by grammar point and five review worksheets. Where there are several worksheets that focus on the same grammatical area, they are ordered from simple to complex so they can be used independently or in sequence.

There are two main types of worksheet: *contextualised worksheets* and *problem-solving worksheets*. The contextualised worksheets provide a story, situation or game that gives the learners the opportunity to practise using the structure in an appropriate context. The problem-solving worksheets take a cognitive approach. They provide activities that help the learner arrive at a fuller understanding of the meanings, formation and rules of the use of the structure. They are identified by this symbol: ▼?.

Using Grammar Activities 1 in class

We use grammar activities both for grammar presentations, whether fresh or remedial, and for quick review activities. When using a worksheet for presentation, before giving out the exercise, we start by introducing the topic or situation, we build up the language together with the class, and finally we give the exercise out for written consolidation. The topic or situation can be introduced in a number of ways: by drawing the picture on the board or showing the picture(s) around the class; by writing key words on the board; or simply by describing the situation. To build up the language we ask questions about the picture(s) to establish who is involved, what they are doing, and what they might be saying, or what is being said about them. We invite as many class suggestions and ideas as possible, correcting the learners' use of the structure where necessary. When everyone has had the chance to hear everyone else's ideas, the class can practise the structure. They do this by pretending to be the people in the picture(s) or by remembering what the class has said. Finally we give out copies of the exercise for the class to fill in from memory.

We use the problem-solving activities with classes that have already used the structure in a limited context and could benefit from thinking about it more widely and more intensively. We do this some time after the initial presentation, usually on a different day, or with a class that needs a review only. We give the class one or two examples of the structure and ask for ideas on how it is different from a similar structure (for example, *a/the*, simple/continuous, *if we go/went now*, etc.) or if they can spot mistakes in it. The answers can lead to a short discussion of what the structure means and how it is used. We then give out copies of the exercise for the learners to discuss and complete in groups.

Either the contextualised or the problem-solving exercises can be used for quick review as a five- or ten-minute activity at the beginning or end of a class. This not only reviews the structure, but is also a good way of breaking up the lesson and changing pace.

The last four *Review worksheets* are intended as review or diagnostic units. Each one contains exercises on a variety of structures that are covered more thoroughly elsewhere in the book.

We hope that both you and your students enjoy using this book and that it also gives you ideas for exercises of your own.

2 Adjectives with -ed and -ing 1

Decide which of the words in brackets completes each of the sentences. Put the correct word into the puzzle to discover the word hidden in the centre of the puzzle.

Example:
   I was very __amused__ when I saw the play. (*amused/boring*)

1 I felt really _____ to hear about your success. (*thrilled/exciting*)

2 That book you gave me was very _____ . (*excited/amusing*)

3 He felt _____ about what they told him. (*confused/worrying*)

4 The journey from Australia was really _____ . (*amazed/tiring*)

5 What's the most _____ experience you've ever had? (*embarrassed/frightening*)

6 They were _____ by your news. (*horrified/thrilling*)

7 All the guests were completely _____ by the awful food. (*disgusted/revolting*)

8 His wife was _____ when he told her he was leaving. (*shocked/amazing*)

9 What you've just told me is very _____ . (*surprised/confusing*)

10 You're a very _____ person; I never thought you would do anything like that. (*astonished/surprising*)

11 The details of the accident were _____ . (*frightened/horrifying*)

© Macmillan Publishers Limited 1994.

Adjectives with -ed and -ing 2

A Make an adjective from each of the verbs in the box to say how each of these people feels.

> frighten   bore   exhaust   excite

1 2 3 4

He feels _frightened_   They feel _____   They feel _____   She feels _____

B Decide which comment was said by each of the people above. Write the number next to the comment.

a) I couldn't even look at the scenes with that terrible monster. ☐
b) Once I started reading I just couldn't put it down. ☐
c) I never learn anything new. I almost fall asleep every time. ☐
d) We left Sydney at 8.00 yesterday. The whole thing took nearly 40 hours. ☐

C First decide which of the topics below each person is talking about. Write the number next to the topic. Second, complete what each person says about the topic by making an adjective from one of the verbs in the box.

> frighten   bore   exhaust   excite

Example:
journey   _1_   It was _very exhausting._
a) novel   _____   It was _____
b) film   _____   It was _____
c) teacher _____   She was _____

D Complete the following sentences by choosing *a* or *b*.

1 She's very interested.   a) I think you should tell her more.
2 She's very interesting.   b) I think you should listen to her more.

3 He's very boring;   a) there are no other children to play with.
4 He's very bored;   b) that's why no one plays with him.

5 When you describe the thing or person which   a) -ed
   produces a feeling or an effect the adjective ends in
6 When you describe how someone or something feels b) -ing
   or is affected the adjective ends in

4 Adverbs of time
since, for, ago

A You can complete the sentence I've been here ... with the 12 words and phrases in the box. However, sometimes you need to use for before the phrase, and sometimes since. Decide which side of the scales to put each phrase on. The scales must balance with exactly 52 letters on each side.

| quite a while | he was born | over a year | Saturday | ages | nine months |
| two years | last weekend | six minutes | June | four o'clock | you arrived |

SINCE: F O U R O C L O C K

FOR: S I X M I N U T E S

Put *for* or *since* in the correct sentence.

a) The words under _____ all say **when** you got here.
b) The words under _____ all say **how long** you've been here.

B Here are some short excerpts from newspapers. Complete the sentences with *for*, *since* or *ago*.

HIGHEST UNEMPLOYMENT FIGURES 1 _____ THREE YEARS.

INFLATION NOW AT ITS HIGHEST POINT 2 _____ 1987.

SHOCK! Superstar admits, 'Yes, I got married in secret two days 3 _____.'

Man sent to prison 4 _____ twenty years.

Winner speaks. 'Three days 5 _____ I was still working at the factory; now, 6 _____ my win, I'm the happiest person alive.'

© Macmillan Publishers Limited 1994.

PHOTOCOPIABLE

Articles 1
use of *a* and *the*

In sections A, B and C put either *a* or *the* in each space.

A

There's __a__ town in Italy called Pompeii. It stands near 1 _____ volcano. In 79 AD 2 _____ volcano erupted and it destroyed 3 _____ town and killed nearly all 4 _____ people who lived there.

B

One day 1 _____ young prince arrived at the castle of King Ottar and fell in love with the king's youngest daughter, who was very beautiful. 'You can only marry my daughter,' said 2 _____ king, 'if you can recognise her, and you must marry the woman you choose.' 'That's easy,' said the prince, and King Ottar put all his daughters behind 3 _____ wall that had 4 _____ space at 5 _____ bottom, so 6 _____ prince could only see seven pairs of feet, and the feet all looked 7 _____ same. Suddenly, one of 8 _____ feet moved and so 9 _____ prince said 'That is 10 _____ woman I love.'

Unfortunately, it was not; it was King Ottar's eldest daughter who was not at all beautiful, but the prince had to marry her. In fact, she was extremely intelligent and had a good sense of humour, so that very soon the prince did fall in love with her and they lived happily ever after. 11 _____ moral of this story is that love is 12 _____ very unreliable thing.

C

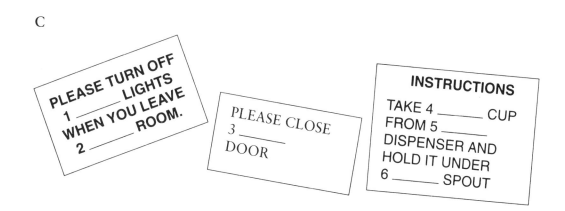

PLEASE TURN OFF 1 _____ LIGHTS WHEN YOU LEAVE 2 _____ ROOM.

PLEASE CLOSE 3 _____ DOOR

INSTRUCTIONS
TAKE 4 _____ CUP FROM 5 _____ DISPENSER AND HOLD IT UNDER 6 _____ SPOUT

6 Articles 2
use of *a* and *the*

A Which sentence goes with which picture?

1 Would you pass me a bottle, please?
2 Would you pass me the bottle, please?

3 Have you got a hair-drier?
4 Have you got the hair-drier?

5 Could you put this on the shelf, please?
6 Could you put this on a shelf, please?

B Look at the pictures again and write the letters in the correct space in these sentences.

1 In pictures _____, and _____ it is clear which one they are talking about.

2 In pictures _____, and _____ it is not clear which one they are talking about.

C Match the explanations on the left with the examples on the right.

1 She is not talking about any particular one; it isn't relevant or she doesn't know.

2 She doesn't expect him to know which one because she's pointing it out for the first time.

3 She expects him to know which one because she's describing it precisely.

4 She expects him to know which one because they have mentioned it before.

5 She expects him to know which one without describing it (because it is the only one she can mean).

a) Hey, Robert, what's that? It looks like a flying saucer.

b) Turn off the light and look at the sky.

c) Can you reach the large camera on the shelf behind your chair?

d) I think we got at least one good photo of the saucer.

e) Let's send it to a newspaper.

© Macmillan Publishers Limited 1994.

Articles 3
the and zero article

Read the sentences under each picture and add *the* only where necessary.

Example:

A: Did you like them, then?
B: Most of them, but I didn't like ___the___ violent films.

1

A: Let's watch 'Kill The Kid' on TV tonight.
B: No, I don't like _____ violent films.

2

I like _____ peace and quiet.

3

I like _____ peace and quiet.

4

Look at _____ sharks.

5

_____ sharks are _____ fish, but _____ whales aren't; they need air.

6

The biggest problem at the moment is _____ pollution; it is destroying our world.

7

The only thing I don't like about this town is _____ pollution.

8

We know very little about _____ nature of sub-atomic particles.

9

Neolithic people lived very close to _____ nature.

© Macmillan Publishers Limited 1994.

8 Comparing 1
comparatives with -er and more

A What is the difference between these things? Write a sentence about each pair using an adjective from the box with -er or more.

| intelligent (loud) dangerous precious big easy sweet |

Example:
a shout and a whisper
A shout is louder than a whisper.

1 diamonds and pearls
_____

2 a mountain and a hill
_____

3 people and monkeys
_____

4 phoning and writing a letter
_____

5 chocolate and fruit
_____

6 a lion and a cat
_____

B What do the verbs in *italics* mean? Complete each sentence using an adjective from the box with -er or more.

| good/bad   expensive/cheap   hot/cold   (senior)/junior   big/small |

Example:
promote: If someone is promoted, they become ___more senior.___

1 *demote*: If someone is demoted, they become _____

2 *heat up*: If something heats up, it gets _____

3 *cool down*: If something cools down, it gets _____

4 *improve*: If something improves, it gets _____

5 *deteriorate*: If something deteriorates, it gets _____

6 *go up*: If the price goes up, it gets _____

7 *go down*: If the price goes down, it gets _____

8 *expand*: If something expands, it gets _____

9 *shrink*: If something shrinks, it gets _____

PHOTOCOPIABLE

Comparing 2
comparatives with -er and more

Put the adjectives from the box in the correct column and write the comparative.

You must decide if the word
1. adds -er (high → higher)
2. doubles the final consonant (big → bigger)
3. changes y to i (pretty → prettier)
4. adds more (precious → more precious)
5. is irregular (far → further)

---

bored   cheap   flat   pleased   noisy   funny   sad   solid   comfortable   thin
good   short   lazy   expensive   bad   long   (kind)   easy
fragile   surprising   wet   intelligent   dangerous

1
+ -er

high – higher
kind – kinder

2
double letter + -er

big – bigger

3
-y + -ier

pretty – prettier

4
more

precious – more precious

5
irregular

far – further

© Macmillan Publishers Limited 1994.

10 Comparing 3
as ... as

A Look at the picture and complete the sentence using *as ... as*.

1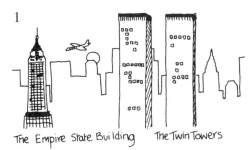

The Empire State Building and the Twin Towers are the highest buildings in New York, but <u>the Empire State Building isn't as tall as the Twin Towers.</u>

2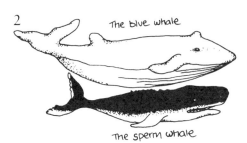

The blue whale and the sperm whale are both famous for being big, but _____

3

The wren and the hummingbird are very small birds, but _____

4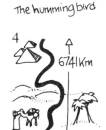

The Nile and the Amazon are the world's longest rivers, but _____

B Read this text about two brothers. Use the adjective in brackets to complete each space. Sometimes you need to use a comparative (*-er, more ... than, as ... as*), and sometimes you don't need to change the adjective.

Children will naturally compare themselves with their brothers and sisters, and this can sometimes be a (dangerous) <u>dangerous</u> thing. There were two brothers called Robin and Rufus. They were both 1 (good) _____ at playing football, but Robin wasn't quite 2 (good) _____ Rufus, so Robin stopped playing football completely.

Robin was three years 3 (young) _____ Rufus, but everyone thought he was the same age because he was nearly 4 (tall) _____ his brother. Of course Rufus was three years ahead of Robin at school because he was three years 5 (old) _____ , but Robin decided that it was because Rufus was 6 (intelligent) _____ him.

Robin began to get very depressed because Rufus was 7 (strong) _____ , 8 (confident) _____ , and 9 (good) _____ him at everything. After a while he just stopped trying.

© Macmillan Publishers Limited 1994.

Comparing 4
as ... as

11

A Read the sentences and put the correct names under the pictures.

1 Frank is older than Peter, but he isn't as old as Vince. Vince isn't as short as Peter, but he's shorter than Frank.

a _____ b _____ c _____

2 The Egyptian vase is not as tall as either the Greek or the Chinese vases, while the longer neck of the Chinese vase makes it more attractive than the others.

a _____ b _____ c _____

B Match each sentence with the correct picture.

1 The animal on the left isn't as small as the one on the right.

2 The animal on the left isn't as big as the one on the right.

3 The animal on the left is just as small as the one on the right.

4 The animal on the left isn't quite as big as the one on the right.

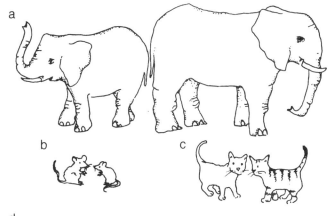

C Join the phrases to make six common English expressions.

1 She ran as fast   a) as the wind.
2 She's as strong   b) as rock.
3 He's as quiet   c) as a mouse.
4 This sweet is as hard   d) as a horse.
5 She's as brave as   e) the hills.
6 It's as old as   f) a lion.

© Macmillan Publishers Limited 1994.

Conditionals 1

first and second conditional

A Write out what each person is saying using the words given. Every sentence is a 'conditional' sentence, but you will need to decide if it is a 'first conditional' – *If it rains I'll stay at home*, or a 'second conditional' – *If it rained I'd stay at home*.

Example:

I have boat like that/I never live on land ___If I had a boat like that I'd never live on land.___

1 you need anything/I get it for you
_____
_____

2 not be raining/I go swimming
_____
_____

3 I can fly/I go to the moon
_____
_____

4 not right size/I bring back
_____
_____

5 I younger/I join you
_____
_____

B You are going to Portsmouth, a seaside town, for the day tomorrow. You are telling George about your plans. Use your thoughts on the left to complete your sentences on the right. In each sentence use either the 'first conditional' or 'second conditional'.

Example:

You want to go swimming.   I _'ll go swimming_
The sea might be warm enough.   if _the sea's warm enough._

1 You want to visit the Science   I _____
   Museum but it isn't open.   if _____

2 You want to buy some new clothes.   If _____
   The shops might be open.   I _____

3 You want to go to the island, but   I _____
   it's too far.   if _____

4 You want to go to the zoo; but only   If _____
   in nice weather.   I _____

5 You want to sail around the harbour;   I _____
   but there won't be enough time.   if _____

© Macmillan Publishers Limited 1994.

Conditionals 2
first and second conditional

13

A Read the four sentences *a, b, c* and *d* and put one letter into each space in the two sentences below.

a) 'If everyone worked together we could make the world a better place.'
b) 'Let's take the plane; if we fly we'll get there faster.'
c) 'Sshh! If you're quiet they won't hear us.'
d) 'If I had more money I'd be happier.'

1 The speaker thinks of sentences _____ and _____ as genuine possibilities.
2 The speaker thinks of sentences _____ and _____ as ideas which may or may not be possible.

B Choose the correct word in column A, and the correct ending in column B and write a complete sentence.

	A	B
Example:	A good business woman would say 'If I *get/got* rich ...	(a) ... I'll move to Florida.' b) ... I'd move to Florida.'

If I get rich I'll move to Florida.

1 A poor man would say 'If I *get/got* rich ...
   a) ... I'll move to Florida.'
   b) ... I'd move to Florida.'

2 A politician running for president would say 'If I *become/became* president ...
   a) ... I'll build houses for everyone.'
   b) ... I'd build houses for everyone.'

3 Someone who knows they will never be president would say 'If I *become/became* president ...
   a) ... I'll build houses for everyone.'
   b) ... I'd build houses for everyone.'

4 An optimist would say 'If I *win/won* a lot of money ...
   a) ... I'll give up work.'
   b) ... I'd give up work.'

5 A pessimist would say 'If I *win/won* a lot of money ...
   a) ... I'll give up work.'
   b) ... I'd give up work.'

6 A woman with twin daughters would say 'If I *have/had* a boy ...
   a) ... I'll call him Rudi.'
   b) ... I'd call him Rudi.'

7 A woman expecting twins would say 'If I *have/had* a boy ...
   a) ... I'll call him Rudi.'
   b) ... I'd call him Rudi.'

C Match each sentence beginning on the left with its ending on the right.

1 You use (if + past) + (would/could)
   a) if you want to suggest that it is not a real possibility.

2 You use (if + present) + (will)
   b) if you want to suggest that it is a real possibility.

© Macmillan Publishers Limited 1994.

14 Conjunctions 1
in case, if, when, unless, as long as

A A friend is giving you some advice about learning English. Use the words or phrases in the box to complete what she says.

| in case   unless   if   as long as   when |

Example:
You won't learn much English ____unless____ you make some British friends.

1 _____ you need a grammar book, I can recommend a good one.

2 Carry a notebook around with you _____ you hear any new expressions.

3 You'll learn the language quite easily just _____ you work hard.

4 I'm sure you'll find a school in London; but here are the names of some others in Cambridge just _____ you can't find one in London.

5 Of course, _____ you study hard you won't make much progress.

6 You'll notice a real difference in your English _____ you get back home.

B You are planning to stay with a British friend. You phone her before your visit. Look at the pictures and complete what she says to you.

Example:
As long as you book early I'm sure _you'll get a plane ticket_.

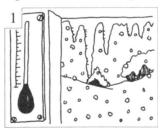
Bring lots of warm clothes in case _____.

We'll be able to go to the park unless _____.

We can try the new Italian restaurant if _____.

I can pick you up at the airport as long as _____.

Bring as much money as you can in case _____.

Conjunctions 2
in case, if, when, unless, as long as

15

A Match each sentence with the correct picture, *a* or *b*.

1 I'll ring you unless I'm busy.
2 I'll ring you if I'm busy.

3 We put them here when they're returned.
4 We put them here if they're returned.

5 He takes an umbrella in case it rains.
6 He takes an umbrella if it rains.

7 As long as you don't drink it, don't worry.
8 If you don't drink it, don't worry.

B Use one phrase from the box each time to complete the signs.

in case   as long as   when   if   unless

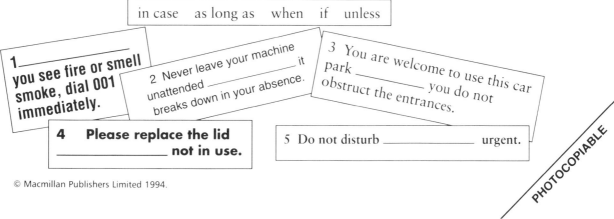

1 _____ you see fire or smell smoke, dial 001 immediately.

2 Never leave your machine unattended _____ it breaks down in your absence.

3 You are welcome to use this car park _____ you do not obstruct the entrances.

4 Please replace the lid _____ not in use.

5 Do not disturb _____ urgent.

16 Countable and uncountable 1
countability

A Match the sentence starters in box A with the nouns in box B. You can only make thirteen sentences. What are they?

A

I've got a …
We've got some …
We haven't got any …
We've got …
We've got a lot of …
There's …
There are some …
We haven't got much …
I haven't got many …

B

dictionary here.
practice exams next week.
food in the house.

B Label each picture with the correct phrase.

plural countable nouns   singular countable nouns   uncountable nouns

C Decide whether a singular, plural or uncountable noun can follow these words and phrases.

Example:
   there is a   _singular noun_

1 there is   _____
2 there are   _____
3 much   _____
4 many   _____
5 a   _____
6 some   _____ or _____
7 a lot of   _____ or _____

© Macmillan Publishers Limited 1994.

Countable and uncountable 2
money, people, work, etc.

17

Choose the correct word or words in each sentence.

Example:

Are/Is there *much/many* cats in England?

How *much/many* money would you like to change?

There *is/are* some people to see you, sir.

John hasn't got a *job/work* at the moment.

You find good *advice/advices* in the strangest places.

Have you got *many/much* warm *clothe/clothes* with you?

Hurry, there *isn't/aren't many/much* time left.

Be careful; there *is/are glasses/glass* everywhere.

Here *is/are* the *new/news*.

Can I give *a/some* food to the animals, Mum?

'Ground Control, we seem to be having some *trouble/troubles*.'

He's thinking about his *trouble/troubles*.

© Macmillan Publishers Limited 1994.

PHOTOCOPIABLE

18 Countable and uncountable 3
is, are, a, much and *many*

Complete the poem using the words in the box.

| is | are | a | much | many |

LIVING IN PARADISE

There __is__ 1 _____ place across the ocean
Where there 2 _____ sand for miles and miles,
There 3 _____ people playing music
And everybody smiles.

You don't need to have 4 _____ money
And you don't need 5 _____ clothes,
There 6 _____ n't very 7 _____ work to do;
Just watch as the ocean rolls.

There 8 _____ space for all who want to come
And as 9 _____ food as you can eat.
There 10 _____ fruit on the trees, and the fish in the sea
Will cook on 11 _____ stone in the heat.

There 12 _____ a lot of time to sit,
Your peace 13 _____ quite assured
In the place where there 14 _____ no problems
Except that everyone is bored.

Countable and uncountable 4

is, are, a, much and *many*

19

A Decide if each phrase in the box is usually used with a singular, plural or uncountable noun and put them in the correct column.

there's some	there's a	there are some
there's	I haven't got a	I haven't got much
I haven't got many	it's a	they're

1 **Singular**	2 **Plural**	3 **Uncountable**
there's a	_____	_____
_____	_____	_____
_____	_____	_____
group		

B Decide if these nouns are singular, plural or uncountable and put them in the correct box above.

| food   people   money   clothes   work   group   luggage |
| advice   children   feet   information   news   traffic   furniture   meal |
| fun   music   place   research |

C Write a sentence to describe each picture. Begin every sentence with *This is …*, *These are …* or *This is a …* and use a word from the box.

| wood   glass   paper   space |

Example: This is wood.

20 Countable and uncountable 5
frequently confused words

A Derek Winters is moving to Swansea to start a new job. He has just arrived in Swansea and has been met at the airport by Sian Williams. Complete the sentences with the correct words from the box. Be careful: sometimes you will need to make the words plural.

> flat   accommodation   hotel   luggage   bag   job   work
> play   theatre   travel   journey   (trouble)   trouble   problem

Williams: Hi. Are you Derek Winters?

Winters: Yes, hello.

Williams: My name's Sian; Sian Williams. Did you have any _trouble_ getting here?

Winters: No, but there is one 1 _____ : not all my 2 _____ has arrived. I sent two 3 _____ but I've only got one.

Williams: Right, we'll go to information.

Did you have a good 4 _____ ? I expect it was lovely flying over the mountains.

Winters: I'm afraid I didn't see them: I get 5 _____ sick so I spent most of the flight with my head in a paper bag.

Williams: Oh dear. You'll feel better soon. When do you start 6 _____ , do you know?

Winters: Not until Wednesday. By the way, what's your 7 _____ ?

Williams: I'm the coordinator between Research and Quality Control, so we'll be seeing quite a lot of each other. Have your got your 8 _____ sorted out?

Winters: Yes. I'm staying at a 9 _____ for a week, and then I'm moving into a 10 _____ that I've just bought. Is there much to do in Swansea in the evenings?

Williams: Well, there's a good 11 _____ on this evening if you're interested in 12 _____ .

Winters: Yes, that's a good idea. Where is it?

Williams: Your hotel will have all the information, but if you have 13 _____ finding out, just give me a ring.

Winters: Right, I will, thank you very much.

B Use the words in the box from A to complete these sentences.

Employment
1 If you're in _____ , you have a _____ .

Holidays
2 If you need _____ , there's a _____ round the corner.

3 He arrived with so much _____ that I had to carry five _____ for him.

Entertainment
4 If you enjoy _____ , there's a good _____ on tomorrow night.

© Macmillan Publishers Limited 1994.

Futures 1
will and *going to*

21

A You are on holiday with a friend. Decide which reply is appropriate to what your friend says to you.

Your friend	You
1 Have you any plans for this evening?	a) Yes, I'll write some postcards. b) Yes, I'm going to write some postcards.
2 In that case, I think we should stay in a hotel tonight.	a) Good idea, it'll be more comfortable than the tent. b) Good idea, it's going to be more comfortable than the tent.
3 I'm too tired to drive any further!	a) OK, I'll drive. b) OK, I'm going to drive.
4 Oh no! Look at the petrol gauge!	a) Yes, I think we'll run out of petrol! b) Yes, I think we're going to run out of petrol!
5 This backpack is so heavy I can hardly carry it!	a) Shall I help you? b) Am I going to help you?
6 The sea looks really rough. Do you still want to take a boat tomorrow?	a) No, if it's rough I think I'll be sick. b) No, if it's rough I think I'm going to be sick.

B Read your friend's comments on the left and then complete your answers using *will/shall* or *be going to* each time.

Example:
This tent looks really unsafe!	Yes, be careful, I think it *'s going to* fall down!
1 I can't reach my back to put this sun-cream on!	Don't worry, I _____ help you.
2 Just look at those black clouds overhead!	Well, I'm not going anywhere, I'm sure it _____ rain!
3 What are you doing with that hammer?	I _____ put the tent up, of course!
4 I think it might be windy tomorrow.	If it's windy it _____ be too rough to swim.
5 I'm really hungry!	Oh, _____ I start making the dinner?
6 Have you decided what to get your mother?	Yes, I have. I _____ buy her a vase.
7 Can you remember the phone number of the pizzeria?	No, but wait a moment and I _____ look in my address book.

© Macmillan Publishers Limited 1994.

PHOTOCOPIABLE

22 Futures 2
will and *going to*

A Look at the pictures and complete the sentence or conversation with the correct phrase, *a* or *b*.

a) he'll be sick.
b) he's going to be sick.

a) Really? Then I'll go and see it tomorrow.
b) Yes, I'm going to see it tomorrow.

a) I'm going to mend the fence.
b) I'll mend the fence.

B Decide which statement best describes which situation in A above.

1 In situation _____ the speaker predicts an event from strong present evidence.

2 In situations _____ and _____ the speakers have already decided to do something *before* the situations.

3 In situation _____ the speaker thinks something might happen as a result of something else.

4 In situations _____ and _____ the speakers decide to do something *as a result* of the situations.

5 In situation _____ the speaker is offering to do something for someone.

C Use the information from A and B above to match the meaning in box A with the form in box B.

A		B
1 You have strong present evidence.	4 You decide something as a result of the current situation.	will/shall
2 You have decided before.	5 You make an offer to do something.	going to
3 You think something might happen as a result of something else.		

© Macmillan Publishers Limited 1994.

Futures 3

will, going to and present continuous

23

You are staying with a friend. During your stay she asks you some questions. Complete your replies to her by choosing the most appropriate ending for your sentence.

What your friend says: **What you say:**

Example:

- Can I borrow your bike? — Sorry but... → g) I'm just going to use it.

1. Would you like to come to a party this Thursday? — Well, thanks, but actually ...
2. Do you know where you're going next? — Yes, I've already got my ticket and ...
3. Do you know that Paul's in hospital? Seems he gets very few visitors. — No, I didn't know. In that case ...
4. There's a great film on at the Plaza, you know? — Oh really? In that case ...
5. Hey! Want to try some octopus? — Yuk! No thanks, if I try that ...
6. You look ill. Do you feel OK? — Not really, in fact I think ...
7. Where are you going for your next holiday? — I haven't really decided yet, but it's possible ...
8. Are you going out tomorrow night? — Yes, in fact I must let Anna know ...
9. Phone's ringing! — Right ...
10. Phil asked if you'd received his letter. — Yes, I've been thinking about that letter. So tell him ...

a) I'll be sick.
b) I'm going to visit her.
c) I'm going to answer it soon.
d) I'll go to Rome.
e) I'll get it.
f) I'm flying to Rome next week.
g) I'm just going to use it.
h) I think I'll visit him tomorrow.
i) I'm going to be sick.
j) I think Pete's having one too.
k) I think I'll see it tonight.

© Macmillan Publishers Limited 1994.

PHOTOCOPIABLE

24 Futures 4
will, going to and present continuous

A Choose the most natural answer, *a* or *b*.

1. Do you know Amelia is ill?
   a) No. In that case I'll go and see her tonight.
   b) No. In that case I'm seeing her tonight.

2. Have you heard from Paola?
   a) Yes, in fact, I'll have dinner with her tonight.
   b) Yes, in fact, I'm having dinner with her tonight.

3. Do you know if Bruno likes jazz?
   a) Well, I hope so. I'll buy him a CD for his birthday.
   b) Well, I hope so. I'm going to buy him a CD for his birthday.

4. If you don't know what to buy for Ali, why not get him some music?
   a) That's a good idea. I'll get him a cassette.
   b) That's a good idea. I'm going to get him a cassette.

5. I don't want to hear that music again tonight!
   a) Don't worry, when I get in, I'm just drinking a cup of cocoa before bed.
   b) Don't worry, when I get in, I'm just going to drink a cup of cocoa before bed.

B Look at the sentences and decide when they are used. Fill in the box by putting a tick ✓ in the box if you would use the sentence in this situation and a cross ✗ if you would not use it in this situation.

	You've just decided now.	You decided before now.	You made an arrangement with someone before now.
Example: I'll go and see her tonight.	✓	✗	✗
1 I'm having dinner with her tonight.			
2 I'm going to buy him a cassette.			
3 I'm just going to drink a cup of cocoa.			

C Match the beginning of each explanation of future forms with its correct ending.

1. You usually use *will*, for example, *I'll do something*
2. You usually use *going to*, for example, *I'm going to do something*
3. You usually use the present continuous, for example, *I'm doing something*

a) when you have decided to do something before speaking about it.
b) when you decide to do something as you speak.
c) to make it clear you have already decided to do something and made an arrangement.

© Macmillan Publishers Limited 1994.

Futures 5

future simple and continuous

A Kevin and Maheen have just had a new baby son. They are talking about their son 'this time next year', and 'in five years' time'. Use the pictures below to complete what they say about the baby.

Example:  This time next year _he'll be sleeping all night._

 1 In five years' time _____

 2 This time next year _____

 3 In five years' time _____

B You are staying with your friend Kelli. You know that Kelli is very busy so you do not want to disturb her plans but there are four things you would like to do. Complete the questions you ask Kelli.

Example:
I need a stamp.
You: Do you think _you'll be passing the Post Office_ ?
Kelli: Yes, I will, why?
You: Well, could _you get me a stamp, please_ ?

1 I'd like to borrow her bike.
You: Do you think _____ ?
Kelli: No, I won't, why?
You: Well, could _____ ?

2 I'd like to watch a film on TV at 10.
You: _____ ?
Kelli: No, I won't, why?
You: _____ ?

3 I'd like to get a message to Jack.
You: _____ ?
Kelli: Yes, I will, why?
You: _____ ?

C Choose the correct verb form to complete the sentence.

1 You must remind him or he'll *forget/be forgetting*.

2 Will anyone *wait/be waiting* for me when I get there?

3 If you give it to me, I'll *post/be posting* it for you.

4 Just think, next month we'll *live/be living* in New York.

5 Can I take the car if you won't *use/be using* it today?

© Macmillan Publishers Limited 1994.

26 Futures 6
future simple and continuous

A Match each sentence on the left of each box with one of the two explanations on the right.

1 Officials will be waiting at the airport when the plane arrives.	a) Two future events: one will happen just after the other.
2 The president will make a speech when the plane arrives.	b) Two future events which will happen at the same time, but one will start before the other.
3 I'll be making dinner soon; would you like some?	c) A future event which is already planned.
4 I think I'll make dinner soon; would you like some?	d) You decide to do something and then talk about it immediately.
5 I'll be going to the Post Office, so I can post your letter.	e) Offering to do something for someone.
6 I'll go to the Post Office and post your letter.	f) Offering to do something for someone because it suits your own plans.
7 You said you'll be going out later, so can you get me some bread?	g) Asking someone to do something for you without disturbing his/her plans.
8 Will you go out later and get me some bread?	h) Asking someone to do something for you.

B Decide which beginning, *a* or *b*, matches each ending.

1. a) Will you work
   b) Will you be working

   when I come back, tomorrow?

2. a) I'll be talking to John
   b) I'll talk to John

   if you ask me to.

3. a) We'll land at Heathrow in ten minutes,
   b) We'll be landing at Heathrow in ten minutes,

   please fasten your seatbelts.

4. a) I'll make some tea.
   b) I'll be making some tea.

   You look so thirsty!

5. a) I was thinking, if you won't use your computer,
   b) I was thinking, if you won't be using your computer,

   can you lend it to me?

6. a) The bus will be stopping
   b) The bus will stop

   when you ring the bell.

7. a) I'll see the manager
   b) I'll be seeing the manager

   so it's no trouble to ask her for you.

8. a) Will you ring me back later?
   b) Will you be ringing me back later?

   I'm sorry, but I haven't time to talk to you.

C Match each of the correct examples in part B with an explanation from part A.

1 ____ 2 _d_ 3 _c_ 4 ____ 5 ____ 6 ____ 7 ____ 8 ____

© Macmillan Publishers Limited 1994.

Futures 7

will/shall, present continuous, *going to*, future continuous

Look at the pictures and complete what each of the people is saying. They are all talking about the future. Use *will/shall*, *am/is/are*, *going to* or *will be* and a suitable verb in the correct form.

Example:

I'm *going* to a party next Wednesday.

1

_____ I _____ your bag for you?

2

Look at all that smoke. I'm sure it _____ very soon!

3

Sorry, but Tuesday is no good for him. He _____ Mr Tiggs all day.

4

Well, OK if it's a girl we _____ her Alice.

5

If it's no trouble and you _____ to the supermarket anyway, could you get me some milk?

6

I _____ my hair.

7

Look, I've got the tickets! We _____ to Sydney next week!

8

Don't worry, _____ it.

9

_____ the light now?

© Macmillan Publishers Limited 1994.

28 Have something done 1

A Erka is going to visit these places today. Write the five things you think she is going to have done, using a word from the box each time.

| back | jacket | hair | car | eyes | shoes |

Example: 1   2   3   4   5

- **GARRICK'S PARLOUR** – back massage a speciality
- **PAOLO HAIRSTYLES** special offer wash & cut £8
- **Kwick:** shoe repairs while-U-wait
- **RUDYARDS OPTICIAN** Eye tests while you wait
- **WALLIS** – same day dry-cleaning
- **MORRIS** Car servicing: no need to book

Example: _She's going to have her back massaged._

1 _____
2 _____
3 _____
4 _____
5 _____

B Rodney has just moved into a new house. Explain why he has so many bills to pay!

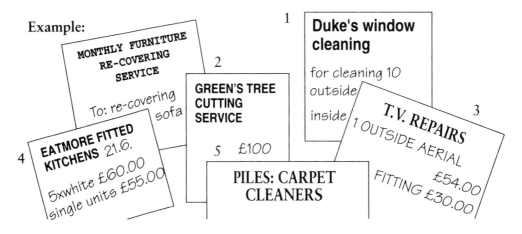

- **MONTHLY FURNITURE RE-COVERING SERVICE** To: re-covering sofa
- **Duke's window cleaning** for cleaning 10 outside inside
- **GREEN'S TREE CUTTING SERVICE** £100
- **T.V. REPAIRS** 1 OUTSIDE AERIAL £54.00 FITTING £30.00
- **EATMORE FITTED KITCHENS** 21.6. 5xwhite £60.00 single units £55.00
- **PILES: CARPET CLEANERS**

Example: _He's had his furniture re-covered._

1 _____
2 _____
3 _____
4 _____
5 _____

PHOTOCOPIABLE

© Macmillan Publishers Limited 1994.

Have something done 2

A Match each sentence with the correct picture, *a* or *b*.

a

1 She's plaited her hair.
2 She's had her hair plaited.

b

a

3 He has the paper brought.
4 He brings the paper.

b

B Here are some adverts in a local shop window in Britain. Which of the adverts are from people who want to have something done for them? _____

a
```
MOTHER REQUIRES SOMEONE
TO TAKE CARE OF CHILDREN
2 HOURS PER DAY     26591
```

b
```
FRIDGE FOR SALE
   ONLY £35
  25 Lakley Drive
```

c
```
    HOUSES
DECORATED VERY
 CHEAP PRICES
 Tel 51592 EVES.
```

d
```
 PIANO - ALMOST
NEW. HARDLY USED
     £2,000.
```

e
```
HAIRDRESSER - ANY
TIME - ANY STYLE
RING SHIRLEY 26492
```

f
```
GARDENER NEEDED
2/3 HOURS EACH
WEEK
51381
```

C Now complete the sentences that the people advertising might say about their adverts, using a verb from the box.

| decorate   do   take care of   do |

Example:
Advert a: I'd like to have my _children taken care of._

1 Advert f: I'd like to have my _____
2 Advert c: Why not have your _____
3 Advert e: Why not have your _____

© Macmillan Publishers Limited 1994.

30 Indirect questions

A

You are a tour guide for 'Sunshine Holidays'. You are telling a new guide about the questions holiday-makers usually ask you. Put the tourists' questions into the correct form to complete the sentences.

They usually ask questions such as 'Can you tell me ...'

Example: ___if___ ___it___ is ___sunny___ ?

1 _____ _____ _____ is _____ ?
2 _____ _____ _____ is?
3 _____ is _____ _____ _____ _____ ?
4 _____ _____ are _____ _____ _____ ?
5 _____ _____ _____ _____ is?
6 _____ _____ _____ are _____ ?
7 _____ _____ _____ _____ are?
8 _____ _____ _____ _____ _____ is?

B Here are some questions the holiday-makers ask you. Match the beginning of each sentence with its correct ending.

Example:
1 Do you know how old — a) is the church?
2 Excuse me, how far away — b) the church is?

3 Could you tell me where   a) are the nearest shops?
4 Sorry to bother you, but how expensive   b) the nearest shops are?

5 What's the   a) countryside like?
6 Have you any idea what the   b) beach is like?

7 Excuse me,   a) if there's a cinema near here?
8 Do you happen to know   b) is there a theatre near here?

9 Do you think   a) the restaurant open on Monday?
10 Does   b) the cafe closes on Sunday?

PHOTOCOPIABLE

© Macmillan Publishers Limited 1994.

Infinitive and gerund 1
infinitive of purpose

31

A Mavis has just moved into a cottage. It needs a lot of work so she has brought some things to help her. Look at the picture of her cottage and write why she has brought each of these things. Use a verb from the box.

cut   mend
catch   cut down
live in   replace

Example:
nails — *She's brought some nails to mend the fence.*

1 lawnmower _____
2 cat _____
3 axe _____
4 glass _____
5 caravan _____

B Mavis is talking to a friend, Pam, on the phone. Pam is asking her questions. Complete Mavis's answers. Use an item from the box each time.

renovate houses   help   look for a new house   talk to you
move around   renovate   be alone

Pam   **Mavis**

Example:
Why did you buy the cottage?   In order *to renovate it* .

1 But why?   I enjoy _____ .
2 Can you do it all by yourself?   No, I'll pay someone _____ .
3 Won't you get lonely there?   No, I like _____ .
4 And what will you do when   I'll start _____ .
    you've finished the work?
5 Don't you want to settle down?   No, not really; I like _____ .
6 Well, I hope you'll be all right.   I will be, and thanks for ringing; I've
                                                                           enjoyed _____ .

© Macmillan Publishers Limited 1994.

PHOTOCOPIABLE

32 Infinitive and gerund 2

infinitive of purpose

A Use the pictures to answer the questions.

Why is she running?
To catch the bus.

Why has he gone out?
_____

Why has he gone upstairs?
_____

Why have they stopped?
_____

B Look at the question and answers. Put a tick ✓ in the box if the answer is possible and a cross ✗ if it is not.

Why did he go to the dance?

Example:

   To meet Molly. ✓

1 For meeting Molly. ☐
2 For to meet Molly. ☐
3 In order to meet Molly. ☐
4 Because he wanted to meet Molly. ☐
5 So as to meet Molly. ☐
6 To meeting Molly. ☐

C Here is a story called 'A Short Affair with Molly'. Complete the story by matching the first part of each sentence with its correct ending.

Example:

One romantic evening I went to the dance specially — c) to meet Molly.

1 I wanted to ask her
2 She was very happy and said that of course she would
3 So the very next day we went to church
4 For a short time we enjoyed
5 But one day Molly began closing her door so as
6 Then she started going out and
7 Soon, I too was sorry I had ever
8 But when she was out I didn't like
9 So I too went out in order

a) to be alone.
b) being alone.
c) to meet Molly.
d) met Molly.
e) to be married.
f) meeting someone else.
g) to marry me.
h) marry me.
i) to meet someone else.
j) being married.

Infinitive and gerund 3

verbs taking either infinitive or gerund

33

A Tricia works as a diplomat for the Irish government. She has lived in many foreign countries and enjoys her work very much. Her husband, Jim, has always travelled with her, but now he is getting tired of travelling. Tricia has just been offered a new post overseas. Use the verbs to complete what Tricia and Jim say. One of the verbs uses the -*ing* form and one the infinitive with *to* each time.

Tricia	Jim	
Example:		
I really enjoy _travelling_ .	I'd prefer not _to travel_ any more.	TRAVEL
1 There are still many places I'd love _____ .	I just don't feel like _____ any more new places.	SEE
2 I love _____ home in different places.	I really don't intend _____ home in any more countries.	SET UP
3 I know I'd hate always _____ in the same place.	I'd just like _____ in one place from now on.	BE
4 I'd miss _____ different ways of life.	I want _____ more about life in Ireland.	EXPERIENCE
5 I hope _____ a lot of money.	I wouldn't mind not _____ a lot of money.	EARN
6 I couldn't stand not _____ anywhere ever again.	I can't promise _____ with Tricia if she takes this job.	GO
7 I can't imagine myself _____ in one place for too long.	I aim _____ in one place, at least for a while.	STAY
8 I've suggested _____ apart for a while.	I've decided _____ apart from Tricia if she wants to travel more.	LIVE

B Use the verbs in the box to complete the advert.

> give   call   make   provide   deal   spend   sail   book

Can YOU answer 'Yes' to these questions?

Do you enjoy _sailing_ ?
Can you imagine 1 _____ three months on a luxury liner?
If so, we'd like you 2 _____ a holiday with us. We aim
3 _____ the best possible service for our clients, and we promise
4 _____ with all those little worries which can make travel difficult.
We don't mind 5 _____ special arrangements to suit your personal needs.
So don't miss 6 _____ yourself the treat of a lifetime. We think you should decide 7 _____ us now!

© Macmillan Publishers Limited 1994.

34 Modal verbs 1
can, should, must

Look at the pictures and complete the sentences with a word from the box.

can	can	can't	can't	should	should	should	shouldn't
shouldn't	must	mustn't	(mustn't)	mustn't			

Example:

You *mustn't* smoke in the library.

a

I think you 1 _____ take the train; it's faster than the bus.

b

I'm sorry, sir, you 2 _____ buy drinks after 11 o'clock.

c

Jan: We're getting married.
Sam: Congratulations.
Jan: But you 3 _____ tell anyone, it's a secret.

d

If you're worried about your eyes perhaps you 4 _____ see a doctor.

e

I don't think we 5 _____ leave him; it's not fair.

f

You know, you really 6 _____ smoke so much it isn't good for you.

g

Now, you 7 _____ be good while we're away, do everything Grandma says.

h

These are my most precious possessions so you 8 _____ touch them, but you 9 _____ look at them.

i

I'm sorry, sir, you 10 _____ come in without a ticket.

j

You 11 _____ be here without a hard hat.

k

Well if you pay for him then I suppose you 12 _____ take him.

© Macmillan Publishers Limited 1994.

Modal verbs 2
can, should, must

35

Must, mustn't, can, can't, should and *shouldn't* all have several different uses. This unit only looks at how they express obligation, permission and advice.

A   Match the sentences with their meanings.

1 I think you should marry him; I know you love each other.

2 You can marry him if you really love him.

3 You must marry the Duke, for me and for the family.

4 You shouldn't marry him because you don't love him.

5 You can't marry him; he's your brother.

6 You mustn't marry him. If you do I shall never speak to you again.

a) I order you to marry him.

b) I order you not to marry him.

c) I think it's a good idea for you to marry him.

d) I don't think it's a good idea for you to marry him.

e) You are allowed to marry him/I allow you to marry him.

f) You are not allowed to marry him.

B   Write *must, mustn't, should, shouldn't, can* or *can't* in the correct space.

1 _____ is used to say that something is possible

2 _____ is used to say that something is not possible

3 _____ is used to advise someone to do something

4 _____ is used to advise someone not to do something

5 _____ is used to order someone to do something

6 _____ is used to order someone not to do something

C   *Can't, mustn't* and *shouldn't* can often be used in the same situation, but they express different attitudes to the situation and to the person you are speaking to.

Match the three sentences on the left with the three attitudes on the right.

1 You can't smoke in here.

2 You mustn't smoke in here.

3 You shouldn't smoke in here.

a) I'm telling you not to smoke.

b) They don't allow smoking here.

c) I suggest you don't smoke here.

36 Modal verbs 3
must and *have to*

Look at the pictures and complete the sentences with the correct form of *must* or *have to*.

Example: You __mustn't__ play with fire, Jonathan.

1 ... then go and sit down. If you think it's too cold you _____ come.

2 You _____ train that dog, Peter. If you don't, I'll sell it.

3 A: Do I _____ change?
  B: No, it's a direct train.

4 You _____ pull that or the train will stop.

5 You _____ answer the question honestly.

6 You _____ meet us at the pub; you can meet us at the cinema a bit later, and we'll still get in together.

7 You _____ give dangerous toys to young children.

8 I don't understand this cooker either, but I think you _____ push this button here and then set the clock, and then it will turn itself off automatically.

9 John _____ take all his exams this year; he can leave three of them until next June and take them then.

10 Take your shoes off before you come in! How many times have I told you? I don't want to _____ tell you again!

11 You can wear either black or white, but you certainly _____ wear red.

12 I don't _____ go back to the dentist, do I?

© Macmillan Publishers Limited 1994.

Modal verbs 4
must and *have to*

37

A Match each of these sentences with the correct picture.

a) You mustn't get up.
b) You mustn't swim.
c) You mustn't see him.
d) You don't have to get up.
e) You don't have to swim.
f) You don't have to see him.

Example:

You mustn't see him.

1

2

3

4

5

B Decide if these sentences are correct or wrong. Correct the mistakes.

1 You mustn't tell me, I already know; John told me. _____
2 You don't have to take me to the airport; I'll call a taxi. _____
3 You don't have to walk in the middle of the road; it's dangerous. _____
4 If the danger flag is flying, you mustn't go swimming. _____
5 You know electricity's expensive; you don't have to leave lights on all over the house. _____
6 We mustn't play this game, there are other games we can play. Do you like cards? _____

C Write *must* or *have to* in the sentences.

1 If you are using your own authority, you say 'You _____ do it.'
2 If you are reporting another person's authority, you say 'You _____ do it.'

D Write *mustn't* or *don't have to* in the sentences.

1 'You _____ do it' means 'Don't do it'.
2 'You _____ do it' means 'You can do it if you want to'.
3 _____ means there is an obligation or need not to do it.
4 _____ means there is no obligation or need to do it.

38 Passives 1
common signs

A Here are some everyday signs. Match each sign with the place where you would see it.

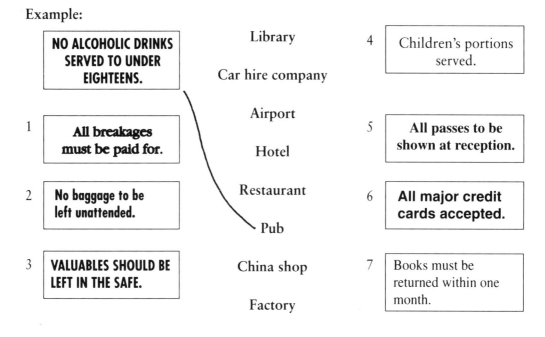

B Complete these signs using a verb from the box in the correct form.

deliver   serve   heel   service   prosecute   fit   park   (accept)

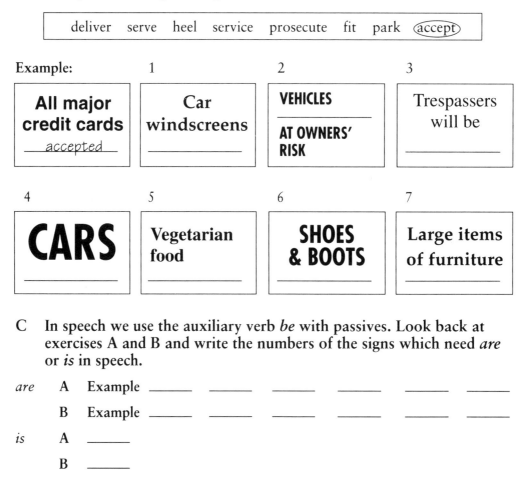

C In speech we use the auxiliary verb *be* with passives. Look back at exercises A and B and write the numbers of the signs which need *are* or *is* in speech.

are   A Example ____ ____ ____ ____ ____ ____

         B Example ____ ____ ____ ____ ____ ____

is   A ____

         B ____

© Macmillan Publishers Limited 1994.

Passives 2
present and past simple, present perfect and modals

39

A Put the *past participles* of these verbs into the correct categories.

> win   teach   forbid   change
> find   (keep)   leave   allow   show   bring   accept

vowel change	ending in -*ght*	ending in -*n*	ending in -*ed*
kept	_____	_____	_____
_____	_____	_____	_____
_____	_____	_____	_____

B Complete the guest information sheet for the Tizzle Hotel by using the verbs from Part A with one of the items from the box.

> is   be   are   has been   were

TIZZLE HOTEL: GUEST INFORMATION

Welcome to the Tizzle Hotel. Here is some information for your comfort and safety.

Example:
Money and other valuables should ___be___ ___kept___ in the hotel safe.

1 All major credit cards _____ _____ .

2 Money can _____ _____ at the bank on the ground floor.

3 It _____ _____ to take hotel towels to the beach, please use your own!

4 Children under 14 _____ not _____ in hotel bars.

5 Tea, coffee and other refreshments can _____ _____ to your room at any time.

6 Non-swimmers can _____ _____ to swim in six easy lessons in the hotel pool.

7 Please remember hotel passes should _____ _____ in all public rooms.

8 Your key should always _____ _____ at the reception desk when you go out.

9 Several valuable items _____ _____ by hotel cleaners last week. If you have lost anything please see the duty manager.

10 This week's bingo prize _____ _____ _____ by Mr Tonks in room 402. Congratulations, Mr Tonks!

40 Passives 3
present and past simple, present perfect and modals

A Match the first part of each sentence in box A with the most natural second part from box B.

A	B
1 The car was serviced	a) every time I see a problem, so it never breaks down.
2 The car has been serviced	b) one day last week.
3 The car is being serviced	c) and the mechanic has just rung to say it's ready now.
4 The car is serviced	d) so I'm afraid we'll have to go by bus today.

B Choose the sentence, *a* or *b*, which can be used in the given situation.

1 The repairs are complete now.
   a) The car is being repaired.
   b) The car has been repaired.

2 Mechanics are working on the car now.
   a) The car is being repaired.
   b) The car is repaired.

3 The car could be broken again now.
   a) The car has been repaired.
   b) The car was repaired.

C Decide which item from the box has been missed out from each headline.

> have been   will be   were   (have been)   are   was   has been

Example:

DEPRESSION HITS TOWN. 100 PEOPLE __ SACKED   *have been*

1 ROAD DEATHS LAST YEAR. 184 PEOPLE __ KILLED.   _____

2 GET YOUR PETROL NOW! PRICES __ INCREASED TONIGHT!   _____

3 ACT TODAY TO PROTECT YOUR WORLD. OVER 1,000 DOLPHINS __ KILLED EVERY YEAR.   _____

4 SHOCK DECISION! PETER JONES __ ELECTED CHAIRMAN. COUNCIL MEMBERS FEAR GREAT CHANGES.   _____

5 COMPANY WORKERS ANGRY AT SECRET SALE. WORKERS CLAIM COMPANY __ SOLD TO OVERSEAS BUYER LAST YEAR.   _____

6 FOG STOPS PLANES. ALL MAJOR AIRPORTS __ CLOSED SINCE 5 PM TODAY.   _____

© Macmillan Publishers Limited 1994.

Passives 4
passive with *should*

41

A These labels are often found in a house. The labels all give advice. Complete them using one verb from column A each time along with the most suitable phrase from column B.

Labels	A	B

Example:

THIS FILM SHOULD NOT BE EXPOSED TO LIGHT.	make	slightly chilled
1 ALL MEDICINES	water	at least one metre apart
2 All cheques	fasten	(to light)
3 THIS HOUSEPLANT	wash	securely to the wall
4 THE SHELVES	keep	payable to British Gas
5 This wine	plant	separately
6 THIS GARMENT	serve	to thaw before serving
7 THE ROSES	allow	frequently
8 The cheesecake	(expose)	out of the reach of children

B Complete the office signs using a verb from the box each time.

remove   park   return   open

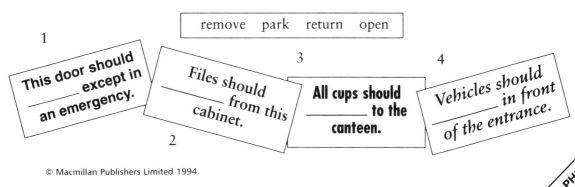

1 This door should _____ except in an emergency.
2 Files should _____ from this cabinet.
3 All cups should _____ to the canteen.
4 Vehicles should _____ in front of the entrance.

© Macmillan Publishers Limited 1994.

42 Past and future

Here are three conversations about a picnic but they are mixed up. Separate them and put them in order. There are two people in each conversation.

Conversation 1

Jodhi: q
Paul: 1 ___
Jodhi: 2 ___
Paul: 3 ___
Jodhi: 4 ___
Paul: 5 ___
Jodhi: 6 ___
Paul: 7 ___

Conversation 2

Sarah: l
Jodhi: 8 ___
Sarah: 9 ___
Jodhi: 10 ___
Sarah: 11 ___
Jodhi: 12 ___
Sarah: 13 ___
Jodhi: 14 ___

Conversation 3

Madha: b
Sarah: 15 ___
Madha: 16 ___
Sarah: 17 ___
Madha: 18 ___
Sarah: 19 ___

a) **Sarah:** We took a picnic.
b) **Madha:** Hi Sarah, what did you do last weekend?
c) **Sarah:** Oh, Brighton's nice. Where are you having lunch?
d) **Jodhi:** Yes, of course you can.
e) **Sarah:** I went to Brighton with Paul and Jodhi.
f) **Jodhi:** We're taking a picnic.
g) **Sarah:** So, when are we leaving?
h) **Sarah:** We left at nine o'clock.
i) **Jodhi:** Paris is too far; why don't we go to Brighton?
j) **Sarah:** I like picnics. Can I come?
k) **Jodhi:** We're leaving early; at eight o'clock.
l) **Sarah:** Hi Jodhi, what are you doing this weekend?
m) **Paul:** All right; Brighton. What time shall we leave?
n) **Paul:** Let's go to Paris.
o) **Jodhi:** Let's leave early; at eight o'clock.
p) **Madha:** And where did you have lunch?
q) **Jodhi:** Hi Paul, what shall we do this weekend?
r) **Jodhi:** We're going to Brighton.
s) **Madha:** Oh, Brighton's nice. When did you leave?
t) **Jodhi:** Let's take a picnic.
u) **Paul:** Yes, that's fine by me.
v) **Paul:** Good idea, and where shall we have lunch?

Past and present
questions

A Decide which question, *a* or *b*, matches the picture.

a) How fast did you travel?
b) How fast were you travelling?

a) What do you read?
b) What are you reading?

a) Did you get married in church?
b) Have you got married in church?

a) Have you met my mother-in-law?
b) Have you been meeting my mother-in-law?

B You are interviewing Tom King, a European cycling champion, about his sport. Look at his answers and finish the questions you ask him using a verb from the box.

| cycle   start   teach   have   (ask)   cycle   cycle   hurt   enjoy |

           You   **Tom**

Example:
   Do you mind if I ___ask you___   No, that's fine, please go ahead.
   a few questions?

1 How long _____   Oh, ever since I was a child. Even
   _____ for?   when I was young I used to get on my
                                          bike first thing in the morning.

2 When _____   When I was about six years old, I
   cycling?   think.

3 Who _____   Well, it was my father who gave
   to cycle?   me my very first lessons.

4 How often _____ ?   Usually at least once a day.

5 When _____ ?   Normally first thing in the morning.

6 Do _____ still _____   Yes I do, I still love it.
   cycling?

7 _____ ever _____   Just once; I crashed into the back
   an accident?   of a car.

8 _____ you _____ ?   No, not badly hurt.

© Macmillan Publishers Limited 1994.

44 Past perfect and past simple 1

John and Pete have both recently been burgled. Here are two conversations describing what happened to each of them. Separate them and put them in order.

Conversation 1

When John came home he found the burglars still in his house.
Alex: I hear you were burgled the other day, John. Did you see the burglars?
John: Yes, I did.
Alex: _____c_____
John: 1 _____
Alex: 2 _____
John: 3 _____
Alex: 4 _____
John: 5 _____

Conversation 2

When Pete came home he found his house empty.
Lynn: I hear you were burgled the other day, Pete. Did you see the burglars?
Pete: No I didn't; I got home later.
Lynn: _____g_____
Pete: 6 _____
Lynn: 7 _____
Pete: 8 _____
Lynn: 9 _____
Pete: 10 _____

a) Yes, I did, and I found someone had been looking through my papers.
b) Did you go up?
c) How did you know there was someone there?
d) Did you go up?
e) Yes, when I looked through the bedroom window I saw someone taking my car.
f) Well, they left footmarks on the carpet so I realised someone had been upstairs.
g) How did you know someone had been there?

h) How awful! Was there anyone else there?
i) Yes, I did, and I found someone looking through my papers.
j) Yes, when I looked through the bedroom window I saw someone had taken my car.
k) Well, first of all, I heard a noise, and I realised there was someone upstairs.
l) How awful! Had they done anything else?

© Macmillan Publishers Limited 1994.

Past perfect and past simple 2

45

A Match each sentence with the correct picture, *a* or *b*.

1 She left when he arrived.
2 She had left when he arrived.

3 She had been swimming when they saw her.
4 She was swimming when they saw her.

5 It had been raining when he went out.
6 It was raining when he went out.

7 Ray had an accident when he came home.
8 Ray had had an accident when he came home.

B Match each sentence with its correct meaning.

1 He had dinner when we arrived.
2 He was having dinner when we arrived.
3 He had had dinner when we arrived.

a) He was in the middle of dinner when we arrived.
b) He finished dinner before we arrived.
c) We arrived and then he started dinner.

C Decide which two of the sentences mean the same thing in each case.

1. a) He had finished work when I got there.
   b) He finished work when I got there.
   c) He finished work before I got there.

2. a) He had just had a bath when I called.
   b) He was having a bath when I called.
   c) He was in the bath when I called.

3. a) She was ill when I last saw her.
   b) I last saw her after her illness.
   c) She had been ill when I last saw her.

4. a) She spoke and then I sat down.
   b) I sat down when she'd spoken.
   c) I sat down when she spoke.

5. a) They had been arguing when I met them.
   b) They were arguing when I met them.
   c) I saw and heard them arguing.

6. a) He learnt to knit before he was seven.
   b) He had learnt to knit before he was seven.
   c) He had been learning to knit before he was seven.

© Macmillan Publishers Limited 1994.

46 Prepositions
prepositions after certain words

A Look at this short extract from a telephone conversation.

A: I'm thinking.
B: What about?

Make ten similar extracts from conversations by joining each sentence in a speech bubble with the correct reply. You must make sure that none of the telephone lines cross!

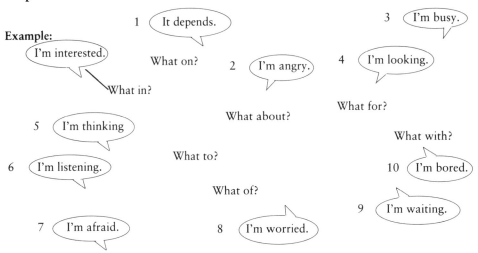

B There is a two-letter preposition missing from each sentence. Use each letter from the word square once to complete the sentences. You can read words horizontally → and vertically ↓.

Example:
He's interested _in_ modern art.

1 I'm really bad _____ making decisions.
2 They were very kind _____ me.
3 She had great difficulty _____ getting here.
4 I'm not very keen _____ the idea.
5 What did you spend all your money _____ ?
6 I've no idea what the solution _____ the problem might be.
7 What are you afraid _____ ?
8 It depends _____ the time of day.
9 What do you think _____ having a party here?
10 Is there any chance _____ seeing you again?
11 In addition _____ that, I don't really understand the problem itself.

O	N	O	F	T	O
I	N	O	O	A	T
O	T	N	F	T	O
N	O	O	F	I	N

© Macmillan Publishers Limited 1994.

Present perfect

A Find out the name of the 'Man of the Year' by completing the sentences and putting the missing words in the puzzle.

'Ladies and gentlemen, please welcome **** **** who we have ... as our Man of the Year. He has 1 ... many interesting things in his life. He is a person who has always 2 ... a lot of time to his work. In his life he has 3 ... many popular books. He has, of course, also 4 ... several films and 5 ... in many plays. During his life he has 6 ... many countries in the world, and has 7 ... seven different languages. We are very happy that he has 8 ... our prize tonight and we wish him many more successes in the future.

Example: C H O S E N

B Look at the pictures and then answer the questions using the words in the box.

tear   disconnect   steal   break   (knock over)

What have the burglars done?

Example: They've knocked over the table.

1 _____
2 _____
3 _____
4 _____

© Macmillan Publishers Limited 1994.

48 Present perfect and past simple 1

A Choose the correct sentence or phrase for the situation.

Example:
Susie: ... well what about yesterday?
    a) Alex: Well, I haven't done anything special.
    (b) Alex: Well, I didn't do anything special.
Susie: That's a pity.

1 Teresa: Can you come to the pub?
    a) Mary: No, I've just washed my hair.
    b) Mary: No, I washed my hair.
Teresa: What a shame, maybe you can join us later.

2 Juan: Why couldn't you come to the pub last week?
    a) Alice: I've washed my hair.
    b) Alice: I washed my hair.
Juan: What a shame, maybe you can join us this week.

3 Matthew: I love travelling.
    a) Francesca: Really? Have you ever been to Paris?
    b) Francesca: Really? Did you ever go to Paris?
Matthew: Oh yes, several times.

4 Satoshi: I lived in the south of France for a year.
    a) Bob: Really? Have you ever been to Paris?
    b) Bob: Did you ever go to Paris?
Satoshi: Oh yes, several times.

5 Ivan: That's my fiancée.
    a) Mika: Really? How long have you been engaged?
    b) Mika: Really? How long were you engaged?
Ivan: Oh, quite a long time.

6 Corrie: That's my ex-fiancé.
    a) Roger: Really? How long have you been engaged?
    b) Roger: Really? How long were you engaged?
Corrie: Oh, quite a long time.

B This is an excerpt from a tennis championship commentary. Complete the commentary using the verbs in brackets in the present simple, the present perfect or the past simple.

And now Donna Scarlatti ____plays____ (play) Barbara Schmidt. Donna, now nineteen, 1 _____ (start) playing when she 2 _____ (be) four. She first 3 _____ (train) with her father, but since his death five years ago, she 4 _____ (train) with the famous Mirenda Merlinghetti.

Donna 5 _____ (play) in some of the most important tennis tournaments of the last four years, but this 6 _____ (be) the first time she 7 _____ (play) at Wimbledon. Oh look! Someone 8 _____ (throw) down a bunch of red roses to her from the crowd. She 9 _____ (be) a very popular player this year, even though most of the crowd 10 _____ (not see) her play before. And now they are about to begin ...

Present perfect and past simple 2

A Match the beginning of each sentence, with its correct ending, *a* or *b*.

1 We got married
2 We've been married

a) since 1986.
b) in 1986.

3 Dinosaurs
4 Many of today's diplomats

a) lived in many parts of the world.
b) have lived in many parts of the world.

5 The arrival of Don Cortes
6 The invention of computers

a) has had a dramatic effect on the modern world.
b) had a dramatic effect on the old Aztec world.

7 This is the first time
8 That was the first time

a) we met.
b) we've met.

B Here are some notes on the use of the present perfect and the past simple. Write the numbers of the notes in the correct part of the notebook.

Example:
to talk about events in the lives of dead people or animals.

1 with *since* and a time reference to say when something, which is still happening, started.

2 to talk about an event which has a present result.

3 to talk about an event which happened at a specific time in the past.

4 to talk about an event which you introduce by saying, 'this is the first time …'.

```
PRESENT PERFECT =

I've done

You often use the present
perfect

___ ___ ___
```

```
PAST SIMPLE =

I did

You often use the past
simple

Example ___
```

C Here are some statements about Britain. Correct any of the verbs in *italics* which are incorrect.

Example:
Queen Victoria *has lived* in Britain.   ____lived____

1 Britain *was* a member of the EC since 1973.   _____

2 Shakespeare *has written* many plays.   _____

3 Queen Elizabeth II *has visited* the United States in 1991.   _____

4 This is the first time since the ice age that Britain *was joined* to France.   _____

5 Margaret Thatcher *has been* the first British woman prime minister.   _____

6 The British currency *has been decimalised* in 1971.   _____

50 Present perfect and past simple 3

A Hans is visiting Britain. He has written the letter below to one of his friends. There are six mistakes in Hans' letter. Correct Hans' mistakes. The first one has been done for you.

Liverpool, Sunday

Dear Henry,

Well, I ~~have~~ arrived here in Liverpool last week. So, I've been here since about nine days now. I've already seen a lot of things, but unfortunately, I haven't gone to London yet. Last night, I've seen a very interesting film. It's been about life in Scotland. I enjoyed it very much. As you can see, my English has already improved. I've learnt so much in a short time. I'm writing to you tonight as I can't go out because I'm waiting for a phone call which didn't come yet. Well, it seems a long time since I saw you, I hope you haven't missed me too much!

With very best wishes,

Hans

B A week later Hans writes a second card to the same friend. Complete his card using the verbs in the box; some verbs are used more than once.

| make   have   give   meet   get   not speak   fall   be   ask   happen |

Dear Henry,

I hope you __got__ my first card last week. A lot 1 _____ since I wrote to you, so much that, in fact, this is the first free moment I 2 _____ to write to you. I 3 _____ an accident about a week ago while playing football. As a result I 4 _____ in hospital since then! I'm enjoying myself here because I 5 _____ a lot of new friends and I 6 _____ a word of German since I came here which, of course, is great for my English. On my first day here I 7 _____ a nurse called Gloria and I 8 _____ in love with her almost immediately. I 9 _____ her to marry me, and she's going to give me her answer tomorrow. As you can see, the last few days 10 _____ very exciting for me. I'll write to you again after Gloria 11 _____ me her answer.

With all good wishes,

Hans

© Macmillan Publishers Limited 1994.

Present perfect and past simple 4

51

A Use the time expressions on the right to make fourteen sentences. The first one has been done for you.

I haven't been to Brighton … I didn't go to Dublin …	1 today 2 for a while 3 this winter 4 for a week 5 yesterday 6 three days ago 7 recently 8 since Tuesday 9 up to now

B Choose the sentence, *a* or *b*, which matches the picture.

1

a) How long did you live here?
b) How long have you lived here?

2

a) Where have they been?
b) Where did they go?

3

a) I've broken my leg just there.
b) I broke my leg just there.

4

a) Hurry up the taxi arrived!
b) Hurry up the taxi has arrived!

C Match each statement with the person who you think said it.

Example:

The government has introduced a new tax. ———— a) historian
The government introduced a new tax. ———— b) news reporter

| 1 I've been married for six years. | a) divorcee |
| 2 I was married for six years. | b) husband |

| 3 I flew planes every day for thirty years. | a) retired airline pilot |
| 4 I've flown planes every day for thirty years. | b) airline pilot |

| 5 How long did you know Josh? | a) guest at wedding |
| 6 How long have you known Josh? | b) guest at funeral |

| 7 My mother told me not to see him again. | a) eighty-year-old |
| 8 My mother has told me not to see him again. | b) eighteen-year-old |

© Macmillan Publishers Limited 1994.

52 Present perfect and past simple 5

Here are two conversations, but they are mixed up. Separate them and put them in order.

Conversation 1	Conversation 2
Pedro visited Britain last year. He is at home in Spain talking to Sally about his holiday.	Jaime is on holiday in Britain. He is talking to Lisa about his holiday up to now.
Sally: Have you ever been to Britain, Pedro?	**Lisa:** How long have you been in Britain, Jaime?
Pedro: Yes, I was there last year.	**Jaime:** Oh, for about three months now.
Sally: ____d____	**Lisa:** ____j____
Pedro: 1 _____	**Jaime:** 8 _____
Sally: 2 _____	**Lisa:** 9 _____
Pedro: 3 _____	**Jaime:** 10 _____
Sally: 4 _____	**Lisa:** 11 _____
Pedro: 5 _____	**Jaime:** 12 _____
Sally: 6 _____	**Lisa:** 13 _____
Pedro: 7 _____	**Jaime:** 14 _____

a) Well, I started in London, and then I went to the South coast.
b) Sounds as if you really enjoyed your stay. Are you thinking of going back?
c) Only another three days, I'm afraid.
d) How long did you stay?
e) Did you get to many places in that time?
f) Perhaps one day; I had a wonderful time.
g) I was there for three months.
h) Did you like the coast?
i) Did you like the coast?
j) How much longer are you staying?

k) Perhaps one day; I've had a wonderful time.
l) Sounds as if you've really enjoyed your stay. Are you thinking of coming back?
m) Yes, the coastal scenery has been one of the highlights of my visit.
n) Yes, I thought the scenery was great.
o) Well, I started in London, and then more recently I've been to the South coast.
p) So where have you been in this time?

© Macmillan Publishers Limited 1994.

Present perfect simple and continuous 1

A Make two sentences about each picture using the verbs in the box.

(run) fish make paint cook re-paint (win) catch

Example:    1    2    3

He *'s been running.*   She _____   He _____   She _____

He *'s won the marathon.*   She _____   He _____   She _____

B Decide what the people are saying. Use the verb in brackets each time.

1

Do you know *I've been waiting* (wait) for an hour!

2

Hurray! _____ (finish) this report at last!

3

Wow! _____ (drive) 450 kilometres today!

4

I _____ (study) all night long!

5

He _____ (travel) a lot in life.

6

He _____ (travel), but now he's on the way home.

© Macmillan Publishers Limited 1994.

54 Present perfect simple and continuous 2

A Match the beginning of each sentence with its correct ending, *a* or *b*.

Example:

I've lived in Birmingham — a) so that's why you haven't seen me recently.
I've been living in Birmingham — b) and London as well.

1	I've driven	a)	most sorts of cars.
2	I've been driving	b)	most of my life.
3	He's stood there	a)	many times before.
4	He's been standing there	b)	all afternoon.
5	I've read the paper	a)	and there's an interesting article on pollution.
6	I've been reading the paper	b)	so I think I'll take a walk now.
7	She's typed the report	a)	so I can give it to you now.
8	She's been typing the report	b)	so it should be finished by Monday.
9	I haven't slept well	a)	so I really must see the doctor.
10	I haven't been sleeping well	b)	so I'll take a rest this afternoon.
11	I've dug the garden	a)	so I'm covered in mud.
12	I've been digging the garden	b)	and planted all the lettuces.

B Write four sentences using a phrase from both boxes each time.

I've been reading I've read	this book all day. about half this book today. this book, but I haven't finished it yet. this book, but I don't remember exactly when.

1 _____
2 _____
3 _____
4 _____

C Write *present perfect simple* or *present perfect continuous* in the correct sentences.

Example:
When you use the *present perfect simple*, the action is often complete.

1 When you use the _____, the action often continues.

2 You can use the _____ if the action happened at any time.

3 The _____ always refers to an action just before now.

4 You use the _____ when you are most interested in how long something took to do.

5 You use the _____ when you are most interested in the result of the action.

Present simple and continuous 1

A Match each sentence with the correct picture, *a* or *b*.

1 I study here.
2 I'm studying here.

3 It cleans really well.
4 It's cleaning really well.

5 She eats fish.
6 She's eating fish.

7 The water comes out here.
8 The water's coming out here.

B Make questions for each of the answers using the words in brackets.

Example:
(How long/you/work/here) _How long are you working here_ ?   Not long; it's only a summer job.

1 (she/speak/Danish) _____ ?   Yes, sometimes, with her parents.

2 (she/speak/Danish) _____ ?   I guess so. I can't understand a word.

3 (Where/you/stay/ in Manchester) _____ ?   Usually at the airport hotel.

4 (Where/you/stay/in Manchester) _____ ?   I'm not sure; I haven't checked the reservation.

5 (What time/plane/arrive) _____ ?   Normally about 9.00.

6 (What time/plane/arrive) _____ ?   About 9.00 tonight, I think.

© Macmillan Publishers Limited 1994.

56 Present simple and continuous 2

A Make three conversations using a sentence or phrase from each box.

1 **A:** I see Jane's not here this morning.
2 **A:** Has Jane left her job?
3 **A:** Jane's never here during the day, is she?

a) **B:** No, she works in town,
b) **B:** No, she's working in town,

i) but only for a few days.
ii) but she's here in the evenings.
iii) but I'm sure she'll be here later.

B Match the use of the verb *work* in these sentences with the correct description.

1 Jane **works** in town, but she's here in the evenings.   a) an action happening now

2 Jane's **working** in town today, but she'll be here later.   b) a normal habit

3 Jane's **working** in town, but only for a few days.   c) a temporary habit, different from usual

C Find the items from boxes A and B which match the sentences 1, 2 and 3.

1 _____ _____   2 _____ _____   3 _____ _____

	A		B
1 Paul doesn't eat enough.	a)	So I'm sure he's going to feel hungry later on.	i) an action happening now
2 Paul's not eating enough these days.	b)	So I hope he'll start eating again when the weather's cooler.	ii) a normal habit
3 Paul's not eating enough.	c)	That's why he's always been so thin.	iii) a temporary habit, different from usual

D Write *present simple* or *present continuous* in the following sentences.

1 The _____ is used to talk about a normal habit.

2 The _____ is used to talk about a temporary habit, different from usual.

3 The _____ is used to talk about an action happening now.

© Macmillan Publishers Limited 1994.

Present simple and continuous 3
stative and dynamic

57

Complete the sentences using the present simple or present continuous of the verb in brackets. Then put the main verb into the correct place in the puzzle. There are two words hidden in the centre of the puzzle. Find what they are.

Example:
Their parents are away, so he <u>'s caring</u> (care) for the children.

1. You _____ (be) really stupid; stop it!
2. This material _____ (feel) very soft.
3. I'm afraid she _____ (see) someone at present.
4. Can I ring you back? I _____ (have) a shower.
5. Do you think he _____ (enjoy) classical music?
6. He _____ (have) a good, efficient shower in his house.
7. You must _____ (think) very deeply; you haven't said a word for ages.
8. He looks as if he _____ (enjoy) the party.
9. This fish _____ (taste) rather strange.
10. The doctor _____ (feel) his leg; let's hope he doesn't find a break.
11. She _____ (think) it's a very good film.
12. I _____ (see) what you mean.

© Macmillan Publishers Limited 1994.

58 Relative clauses 1
defining relative clauses

The Personnel Manager has just employed a new accountant. He is showing the Managing Director the photographs of all the other applicants for the job and explaining who they are.

Complete the Personnel Manager's sentences using a relative clause in every sentence to identify the people in the photographs.

Example:

answered the advertisement These
<u>are the people who answered</u>
<u>the advertisement.</u>

1 came for an interview These _____
_____
_____

2 shortlisted These _____
_____
_____

3 didn't get back in touch This _____
_____
_____

4 references asked for These _____
_____
_____

5 rejected These _____
_____
_____

6 got the job This _____
_____
_____

PHOTOCOPIABLE

© Macmillan Publishers Limited 1994.

Relative clauses 2
defining relative clauses

A Look at the pictures and read the conversations. Name the people in the pictures.

'Did Sally give the plant to Michiko?'
'No, Michiko's the person who gave the plant and Jorge is the person (who) she gave it to.'

'Which one is Gotam?'
'He's the person who carried Sabrina down the mountain.'
'And Michael?'
'He's the person (who) Steven carried.'

Michiko   1 _____
2 _____   4 _____
3 _____   5 _____

B Read the sentences and answer each question with a name.

Geraldine's the person who told Frederique.

John's the person (who) Min Yao told.

Mrs Roach is the person (who) Mrs Singh interviewed.

David is the person whose umbrella Lydia took by accident.

Example:
Who spoke? _Geraldine_
1 Who listened? _____
2 Who spoke? _____
3 Who listened? _____
4 Who was the interviewer? _____
5 Who was the candidate? _____
6 Who took the umbrella? _____
7 Whose umbrella is it? _____

C Decide if the words *who, me, I* and *whom* are the *subject* or *object* of each relative clause and write *a* or *b* in the correct spaces.

Leo is the person who told me.
1 *who* is _____
2 *me* is _____

Leo is the person (who) I told.
3 *I* is _____
4 *who* is _____

5 You must use *who* if it refers to _____

6 You do not need to use *who* (or *whom* in formal English) if it refers to _____

a) the SUBJECT of the relative clause.

b) the OBJECT of the relative clause.

© Macmillan Publishers Limited 1994.

60 Relative clauses 3
defining relative clauses

Marianna had her fifteenth birthday yesterday. Unfortunately it did not go very well. Here are three lists she made:

A

PRESENTS I RECEIVED

1 Computer: from Uncle Toby
2 Tea-making radio alarm clock: from Mum
3 Earrings: from Paul

B

INVITATIONS TO MY BIRTHDAY PARTY

Peter
Sarah
Abraham
Frances

C

THINGS TO DO ON MY BIRTHDAY

Put up new shelves in my bedroom

Visit fortune-teller

Go to restaurant with Mum and Dad for lunch

AND … man comes to mend the new computer

Use the information in the lists to complete Marianna's letter to her brother, Paul. Complete the sentences using the verb in brackets in a *relative clause*, for example, 'A Parisian is a person *who lives in Paris*' or 'Thank you for *the letter you sent me*'.

Dear Paul,
  I had a terrible birthday yesterday; nearly everything went wrong. The computer <u>Uncle Toby gave me</u> (gave) broke, and the man
1 _____ (came) couldn't understand what was wrong, so I'll have to take it back to the shop. Then the new shelves
2 _____ (put up) fell down immediately. The restaurant
3 _____ (took to) was terrible, and the friends
4 _____ (invited) didn't come. Then in the evening, Peter, one of the friends 5 _____ (asked) phoned and said that the invitation 6 _____ (sent) hadn't arrived in time.

  But there were some good things; Mum gave me a radio alarm clock
7 _____ (makes), and it works! In the afternoon, Dad took me to an old woman 8 _____ (told), and she said that one day I'm going to be a famous actress, but I don't believe her!

  Anyway, thank you very much for the earrings 9 _____ (sent); they are the best present 10 _____ (got) I'm wearing them now. I hope you can come back home soon.

  With lots of love from,

  Marianna

© Macmillan Publishers Limited 1994.

Relative clauses 4
defining relative clauses

61

A Choose the correct ending to these sentences, *a* or *b*.

Example:
A rocking chair is a chair   a) which rocks.
                              b) who rocks.

1 A passenger is anyone in a car   a) which is not driving.
                                     b) who is not driving.

2 You are legally responsible if you are at the wheel of a car
                                     a) which is moving.
                                     b) who is moving.

3 A predator is an animal   a) which kills other animals for food.
                              b) who kills other animals for food.

4 You use *who* (or occasionally *that*)
   a) for people (and for animals you have an affection for).
   b) for things (and animals you have no affection for).

5 You use *which* (or *that*)
   a) for people (and for animals you have no affection for).
   b) for things (and for animals you have no affection for).

B Match the beginnings of these sentences with their endings.

Example:
Cannibals are **people**   a) who **eats** other people.
A cannibal is **a person**   b) who **eat** other people.

1 A reference book is **a book**   a) that **gives** you information.
2 Reference books are **books**   b) that **give** you information.

3 Spiders are **animals**   a) which **has** eight legs.
4 Spiders are **a kind of creature** b) which **have** eight legs.

5 It's not the place; it's the **people**   a) who **comes** here that I don't like.
6 It's the **type of person**   b) who **come** here that I don't like.

C Choose the correct ending for each sentence.

Example:
A pen is something
a) you write on.
b) you write with.
c) you write in.

1 Food is something
   a) who cooks.
   b) you cook.
   c) you cook in.

2 A cook is someone
   a) who cooks.
   b) you cook in.
   c) you cook for.

3 A saucepan is something
   a) who cooks.
   b) you cook.
   c) you cook in.

4 A guest is someone
   a) you cook.
   b) you cook in.
   c) you cook for.

5 A cooker is
   a) someone who cooks.
   b) something you cook.
   c) something that cooks.

© Macmillan Publishers Limited 1994.

Reporting 1
62
past perfect after *I realised, I discovered*, etc.

Yesterday was a bad day for everyone. Match the pictures of what these people did yesterday with what they say today and complete their sentences.

What happened yesterday

a
Oh no! I've missed my train.

b
Oh no! It's just been painted!

c
I hope he's written to me.

d
I've lost my voice.

e
I've been robbed!

f
I've run out of petrol!

What they say today

Example:

   _d_   When I started to sing I realised _I had lost my voice._

1 _____ When I stood up I discovered _____

2 _____ When I got to the station I found _____

3 _____ Then the car stopped and I realised _____

4 _____ I felt something so I looked down and discovered _____

5 _____ Then the post arrived and I hoped _____

© Macmillan Publishers Limited 1994.

Reporting 2
tense changes

63

Here are two people talking about their past. Complete the texts using indirect speech and the words given.

A Samantha: childhood imaginings

When I was a child I used to think that   I was the fastest runner in the world

and that 1 _____ .

I thought 2 _____ .

but I still thought 3 _____ .

B Samuel: a smoker's life

Age 8:	'Smoking is bad for you.'
Age 10:	'I'm never going to start smoking.'
Age 16:	'OK. I'll try it just once.'
Age 17:	'I only smoke at weekends.'
Age 18:	'I can give up any time I like!'
Age 21:	'I've given up!'
Age 25:	'I can't give up. It was a bad idea to start in the first place.'

Example:
   When   I was 8 I thought that smoking was bad for you   .   (think)

1 When _____ .   (promise)

2 When _____ .   (say)

3 When _____ .   (insist)

4 When _____ .   (boast)

5 When _____ .   (declare)

6 When _____ .   (admit)

7 and that _____ .

© Macmillan Publishers Limited 1994.

64 Reporting 3
tense changes

There was a board meeting at Jinks' Drinks plc yesterday. Read what everyone said at the meeting.

Now complete the report of what was said at the meeting. Sometimes two answers are possible.

Example:

Mrs Rye said that our customers _wanted larger cans and they'd pay more for them. / want larger cans and they'll pay more for them._

1 Mr Roberts agreed with Mrs Rye and said that in the survey he _____

2 Mr Rose disagreed with Mrs Rye and Mr Roberts and made the point that surveys _____

3 Finally, Mr Hollis claimed that it _____

Thirty years later, the largest canned drinks company in the world, Jinks' Drinks, owes its success to the decision to increase the size of its cans. The plan was discussed thirty years ago at a historic meeting where:

4 Mrs Rye said that their customers _____

5 Mr Roberts agreed and said that in the survey he _____

6 Mr Rose disagreed with Mrs Rye and Mr Roberts and made the point that surveys _____

7 and Mr Hollis claimed that it _____

© Macmillan Publishers Limited 1994.

Reporting 4
tense changes

65

A Match each sentence beginning on the left with its possible ending(s) on the right.

1 One day an old man called Columbus came into the bar, just here, and said … 2 One day a young man called Columbus came into the bar, just here, and said …	a) he would find a new way to Asia. (*or* he was going to find a new way to Asia.) b) he had discovered the New World. (*or* he discovered the New World in 1492.)
3 I think we should give him ice-cream for dinner tomorrow … 4 I don't think he likes ice-cream any more although …	a) he said he liked it. (*or* he said he likes it.) b) he said he had liked it. (*or* he said he liked it as a child.)
5 'I'm 100 years old today, and the doctors said I'll live … 6 'I'm 100 years old today, and the doctors said I'd live …	a) until I was 55, if that!' b) until I'm 120!'
7 *She said she had met him* means … 8 *She said she will meet him* means … 9 *She said she would meet him* means …	a) she is still waiting to meet him. b) she intended to meet him after saying this. (Perhaps she did meet him. Perhaps she forgot. Perhaps she is still waiting.) c) she met him before she said this.

B Read these six statements and their examples. Put a tick ✓ in the box if the statement is true. If it is false, put a cross ✗.

1 ☐ If something was said in the past, it is normal to report all of it in the past, for example: 'My name's Tracy.' → 'She <u>said</u> her name <u>was</u> Tracy.'

2 ☐ If something is still true you can show this by not changing the verb into the past, for example:
'The sun is hotter than it used to be.' → 'She said the sun <u>is</u> hotter than it used to be.'

3 ☐ Even if the situation is different now, you can still use present and future tenses, for example:
'Neil Armstrong will land on the moon next year.'(said in 1968) → 'They announced that Neil Armstrong <u>will land</u> on the moon the following year.'

4 ☐ If Sue described an event that happened at the time she spoke, you use the past simple to report it for both verbs, for example:
'I'm a spy.' → 'She <u>said</u> she <u>was</u> a spy.'

5 ☐ If she described an event that happened before she spoke, you often use the past perfect to report it, for example:
'I was a spy.' → 'She said she <u>had been</u> a spy.'

6 ☐ But if she said *when* the event happened, the past perfect is often unnecessary, for example: 'I was a spy until 1989.' → 'She <u>said</u> she <u>was</u> a spy until 1989.'

© Macmillan Publishers Limited 1994.

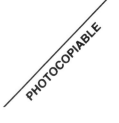

66 Substitution words and others
proforms, particles, etc.

A Find the words missing from the sentences in the word square. You must use every letter in the word square at least once. You can read words horizontally →, vertically ↓ and diagonally ↘.

Example:
I don't know yet. I'll need to think about ___it___ .

1 This is delicious juice, is it OK if I have _____ more?
2 I hear John's coming, can I come _____ ?
3 I don't like tea _____ coffee.
4 Just take the _____ you like best.
5 She's not going because she doesn't want _____ .
6 These are fine, but I'd prefer some of _____ .
7 In the end, he went by him _____ .
8 They bought those books so I hope they enjoy _____ .
9 It'll be sunny, at least I hope _____ .
10 Sorry, there isn't _____ tea left.
11 I didn't see Jerry, and I didn't see George _____ .
12 I suppose I'll have to do it if no-one _____ will.

T	H	O	S	E	E
O	S	O	M	E	I
O	N	E	I	T	T
A	N	Y	L	O	H
E	L	S	E	F	E
T	H	E	M	O	R

B Complete the replies to the questions with one word.

Example:
Is it OK to watch TV? Yes, of course it ___is___ .

1 Do you know if anyone's been to Swansea? — I think Phil _____ .
2 I wasn't at home last night. — That's strange, I thought you _____ .
3 Are there any glasses left? — Yes, I'm sure there _____ .
4 Mary said she'd never met him. — Oh, I thought she _____ .
5 Will you get me a paper? — Yes, of course I _____ .
6 Who gave you that book? — John _____ .
7 Can you come next week? — Yes, I think _____ .
8 I don't know if it's a good idea to go. — Well, I think you _____ .
9 Judy says you speak Greek. — Yes, I _____ .
10 Can I borrow your bike? — Yes, of course you _____ .
11 Don't they mind when you play the drums? — Well, my wife _____ ; she loves it.
12 I wonder if anyone's seen this film before. — Yes, I think I _____ .
13 Don't forget to lock the door. — Don't worry, I _____ .
14 I think it's going to rain. — Oh no, I hope _____ .

PHOTOCOPIABLE

© Macmillan Publishers Limited 1994.

Suggestions 1
How about -ing? Let's ... Why don't we ...? etc.

A Look at the pictures. The speaker is asking for a suggestion or making a suggestion. Complete what he or she is saying.

Example:

Do you feel _like coming_ to a party?

1

How _____ going for a swim?

2

Shall _____ the bus or the train?

3

_____ 's _____ down.

4

Why _____ we _____ for a walk in the park?

5

_____ like to dance?

6

What _____ hiring a video this evening?

7

What do you think we _____ do now?

B Decide which answer goes with each question in part A.

Example:
Not really, I'm afraid. I won't know anyone. _Example_

a) Yes, that's a good idea. My feet are a bit tired. _____
b) You must be joking! It's far too cold in there! _____
c) Well, the bus would be cheaper. _____
d) Why not? It's a lovely day to go out. _____
e) No idea. I think that was the last one. _____
f) Well this one's rather fast for me, I'm afraid. _____
g) Yes, if there's one I haven't seen. _____

68 Suggestions 2
How about -ing? Let's ... Why don't we ...? etc.

A Make ten suggestions or ways of asking for suggestions by using an item from each box.

A	B	C
Shall we How about Why don't we Where shall we What shall we Where would you like Let's	watching a video go watch a video to go do	?

B You are visiting a British friend who wants to know what you would like to do this evening. Decide which four sentences she can say. Put a tick ✓ in the box if the sentence is possible and a cross ✗ if it is not.

Example:
Do we have a pizza? ✗
1 Shall we have a pizza? ☐
2 Are we going to have a pizza? ☐
3 Will we have a pizza? ☐
4 Do you feel like having a pizza? ☐
5 Do you like to have a pizza? ☐
6 What about to have a pizza? ☐
7 Let's have a pizza. ☐
8 Why we don't have a pizza? ☐
9 Would you like to have a pizza? ☐

C Now decide which four answers you can give your friend.

Example:
I prefer not. ✗
1 I'd rather not. ☐
2 I think no. ☐
3 That's a good idea. ☐
4 Yes, we shall. ☐
5 Yes, we do. ☐
6 Yes, let's. ☐
7 Yes, I'd like. ☐
8 I'd love to. ☐

D Use one word from the box each time to complete Hal and Amy's conversation.

| have | having | eat | eating | watch | watching | what | one | that |
| too | do | can't | shall | no | not | | | |

Hal: 1 _____ you feel like 2 _____ out this evening?

Amy: 3 _____ I'm afraid I'd much rather 4 _____ in.

Hal: OK. Then 5 _____ about 6 _____ a take-away and 7 _____ a film?

Amy: Yes, I'd like 8 _____ . Let's 9 _____ the 10 _____ you recorded last night.

Hal: 11 _____ we 12 _____ a bottle of wine 13 _____ ?

Amy: Well, I 14 _____ see why 15 _____ !

© Macmillan Publishers Limited 1994.

Time phrases
present simple after *if*, *unless*, etc.

Look at the pictures and complete each sentence using the verb given. Sometimes you have to use the present simple, sometimes the present perfect.

Example:

Don't get cold, and you must come in if it __rains.__ (rain)

1

Now don't move until I _____ (tell)

2

A: I'm leaving on Monday.
B: Shall I see you before you _____ (go)?

3

Now, everyone shout 'Happy Birthday' as soon as he _____ (come in)

4

Yes, I'll be ready soon; I'm coming as soon as I _____ (get dressed)

5

You can have that one when he _____ (repair)

6

Will you think about me when I _____ (go)?

7

I'll go and ask: wait here till I _____ back. (come)

© Macmillan Publishers Limited 1994.

70 Too and enough 1

A Answer these questions using *too* or *enough*, and an adjective from the box.

| fat | (cold) | far | sweet | hot | old |

Example: Why can't you make ice in a fridge? _Because it isn't cold enough._

1 Why is it dangerous to sunbathe in the Sahara Desert? _____
2 Why would someone ask for more sugar in their coffee? _____
3 Why do people go on diets? _____
4 Why can't people fly to the planet Jupiter yet? _____
5 Why can't children drive? _____

B Complete these sentences using *too* or *enough*, and an adjective and verb from the box.

| bright/look at   (old/vote)   small/see   long/learn |
| expensive/buy   warm/swim in |

Example: If you are 14 years old, you _aren't old enough to vote_ in an election.

1 For most people, diamonds _____
2 In hot countries, the sun _____
3 In winter, the sea _____
4 A one-week course _____ English.
5 An atom _____

C The new managing director of a factory wants to change everything. Complete his sentences with phrases using *too* or *enough*.

This factory must change; the conditions here are terrible. _There are too many_ accidents for four reasons; first, 1 _____ people working in a small area; second, the light is bad, 2 _____ light to see clearly; third, 3 _____ noise for anyone to hear instructions clearly, and fourth, the workers are half asleep because 4 _____ coffee breaks – they must have at least two a day. Moreover, we aren't making 5 _____ money because we haven't got 6 _____ qualified workers and we are losing 7 _____ days through sickness.

PHOTOCOPIABLE

© Macmillan Publishers Limited 1994.

Too and enough 2

A Match each sentence with the correct picture, *a* or *b*.

1 They're very small.
2 They're too small.

3 It's very big.
4 It's too big.

5 I don't know how old he is, but he's very old.
6 I don't know how old he is, but he's too old.

B Is the word in *italics* a *noun*, an *adjective* or an *adverb*?

Example:
There aren't **enough** *people* here to have a game of football.   _____noun_____

1 I can't run **fast** *enough* to catch him.   _____
2 The coffee break isn't **long** *enough*.   _____
3 We haven't got **enough** *time* to have a cup of tea before we go.   _____

C Choose the correct word to complete each sentence.

Example:
It isn't ___wet___ enough.   (wet)/water

1 There isn't enough _____ .

2 I haven't got enough _____ to get up, can you help me?   strong/strength

3 I'm not _____ enough to carry you.

4 We'll buy one when we are _____ enough.   money/rich

5 We'll buy one when we have enough _____ .

6 You've got to build up enough _____ to take off at the end of the runway.   fast/speed

7 You've got to go _____ enough to take off at the end of the runway.

© Macmillan Publishers Limited 1994.

72 Used to

A Match the beginning of each sentence with the correct ending.

Example:
I used to go to school here — c) when I was young in the 1950s.

1. I never used to get up on time
2. I didn't use to understand mathematics
3. This used to be a small town
4. Children used to play outdoors much more
5. I didn't use to eat many sweets
6. I used to live in the countryside

a) until computer games became popular.
b) until I gave up smoking.
c) when I was young in the 1950s.
d) until I bought an alarm clock.
e) before I moved to New York.
f) before oil was discovered here.
g) when I was at school; we had a terrible teacher.

B Matthew used to be Rocky Lee's friend when they were children. Rocky has become a famous pop star and they are not friends any more. Complete Matthew's sentences using *used to* or *didn't use to* and a verb from the box.

(live) be wear play
go climbing play know
think come and watch

I knew Rocky Lee when we were children together, long before he was famous. He was a nice guy. We grew up together.

He ___used to live___ next door to me. He 1 _____ TV with me. At the weekend, we 2 _____ together in the mountains. In the evenings we 3 _____ in a band together. He sang because he 4 _____ the guitar then. He 5 _____ fancy clothes either. He 6 _____ lots of rich people. He 7 _____ my friend. I 8 _____ I was going to be famous too.

© Macmillan Publishers Limited 1994.

Want someone to do something

73

Look at what the people are doing and match the speech bubbles to the correct pictures. Then write a sentence saying what the speaker wants or doesn't want to happen.

a) Can you repair the tap?
b) Please listen!
c) Would you take our photograph?
d) Can you bandage my finger?
e) Could you give me directions?
f) Would you cut the string for me please?
g) Get me down!
h) Let's play football.

Example: d

the patient/the nurse The patient wants the nurse to bandage his finger.

the customer/the cashier

the teacher/the class

the man/the plumber

the tourist/the police officer

the tourists/the waiter

the girl/the boy

the parachutist/the workers

© Macmillan Publishers Limited 1994.

74 Wish 1

past simple

Antonella comes from Italy. She and David got married two months ago and they went to live in David's house in a small village in Scotland. Antonella is not happy. She is sitting at home when her best friend phones her from Italy. Look at Antonella's problems and complete her sentences.

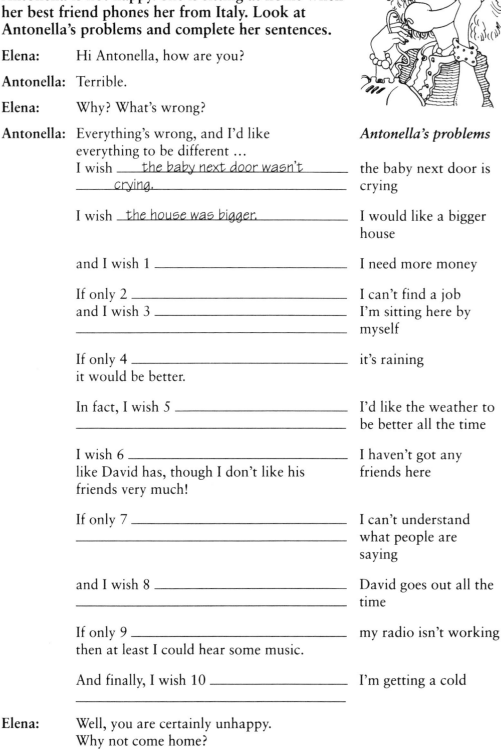

Elena: Hi Antonella, how are you?

Antonella: Terrible.

Elena: Why? What's wrong?

Antonella: Everything's wrong, and I'd like everything to be different …

I wish _the baby next door wasn't crying._ — the baby next door is crying

Antonella's problems

I wish _the house was bigger._ — I would like a bigger house

and I wish 1 _____ — I need more money

If only 2 _____ — I can't find a job
and I wish 3 _____ — I'm sitting here by myself

If only 4 _____
it would be better. — it's raining

In fact, I wish 5 _____ — I'd like the weather to be better all the time

I wish 6 _____
like David has, though I don't like his friends very much! — I haven't got any friends here

If only 7 _____ — I can't understand what people are saying

and I wish 8 _____ — David goes out all the time

If only 9 _____
then at least I could hear some music. — my radio isn't working

And finally, I wish 10 _____ — I'm getting a cold

Elena: Well, you are certainly unhappy. Why not come home?

Antonella: Yes, I think I will; as soon as possible!

Wish 2

past perfect and past simple

A Antonella from Italy has married David from Scotland. They have come to live in Scotland, but Antonella is not happy. She has just been speaking by telephone to her Italian friend, Elena. After the phone call David comes home. Complete Antonella's sentences using *I wish* and the verb in brackets. Notice that she is talking about the past.

David: Hello, Antonella, how are you?

Antonella: I feel terrible. Elena phoned me and I've realised how terrible life is here. Now I want to go home.

David: But we came here because you wanted to.

Antonella: Yes, but now ___I wish I hadn't come.___ (come)

David: You said you wanted to travel, and you didn't want to stay in Italy.

Antonella: Well now 1 _____ (stay) there.

David: But I don't want to go back to Italy.

Antonella: That's all right; I don't want you to come.

David: But we only got married eight weeks ago.

Antonella: And now 2 _____ (get married)

David: Perhaps we need longer to understand each other; we only met twelve weeks ago.

Antonella: And 3 _____ (meet)

David: This is all because Elena phoned, isn't it?

Antonella: Yes, and 4 _____ (phone) two months ago. Goodbye David.

B Read the thoughts on the left and finish the sentence beginning with *I wish ...* . Be careful: some sentences are about the past, and some about the present or future.

Example:

Ian isn't coming to the party.   I wish ___John was coming to the party.___

1 I've spent all my money.   I wish _____
2 I can't drive.   I wish _____
3 I have to go to the dentist.   I wish _____
4 The sun isn't shining.   I wish _____
5 I wasn't there at the end of the party.   I wish _____
6 You haven't got any patience.   I wish _____
7 The wind's blowing hard.   I wish _____
8 I told him he was stupid.   I wish _____

76 Wish 3

past perfect and past simple

A Put these sentences in the correct column in the table.

Example:
   I wish our house was bigger.
1 I wish that baby wasn't crying.
2 I wish I hadn't met her.
3 I wish Rachel didn't go out so often.
4 I wish my radio was working.
5 I wish I had stayed in Peru.

a) Talking about the past	b) Talking about regular things	c) Talking about what is happening at the moment
	I wish our house was bigger.	

B Match the situations on the left with the thoughts on the right.

Example:
   It's raining.

1 It rained in the middle of the barbecue last weekend.
2 It always rains here.
3 I haven't got enough money for a taxi.
4 I didn't have enough money for a taxi.
5 I'm not planning to go to the party because no one has invited me yet.
6 I didn't go to the party because no one invited me.

a) 'I wish I had had more money.'
b) 'If someone invited me I would go to the party.'
c) 'I wish it hadn't rained.'
d) 'I wish it wasn't raining.'
e) 'I wish I had more money.'
f) 'I wish it didn't rain.'
g) 'If someone had invited me I would have gone to the party.'

C There is one mistake in each of these sentences. Find the mistake and correct it.

Example:
   I wish I can fly. ___I wish I could fly.___

1 My house was robbed last year. The money wasn't so important, but I wish the burglar didn't take my grandmother's ring. _____
2 I wish you told me this yesterday. _____
3 This is a beautiful place; I wish we don't have to leave so soon. _____
4 I wish my garden would be bigger, then I could have a garden party. _____
5 I wish I would have seen the end of the film. _____
6 I wish I would have known so I could have told you. _____
7 If your house is smaller it wouldn't be so expensive to heat. _____
8 I wish my boyfriend would be taller. _____

PHOTOCOPIABLE

© Macmillan Publishers Limited 1994.

Word order

77

position of direct object and adverbs, e.g. *very much*

A Look at each sentence and decide where the object of the sentence – the word or phrase on the right – should go. Then write the letter in the rule box below to discover a useful grammar rule.

Objects

Example: I left (d) on Tuesday _n_ .   Moscow
1 Did he lend you _b_ last weekend _n_ ?   very much money
2 Have you _o_ seen _v_ before _t_ ?   St Paul's Cathedral
3 Doesn't she like _e_ very much _i_ ?   holidays by the sea
4 He _a_ always _c_ rides _b_ to work.   his bicycle
5 He _o_ missed _i_ again _a_ this morning.   the train
6 I sent _c_ yesterday _n_ to my daughter.   a letter
7 I _g_ visit _t_ every year _a_ .   my uncle
8 We never _w_ play _j_ on Sundays _r_ because we usually go out.   tennis
9 Don't you _u_ telephone _r_ every week _e_ ?   your parents
10 I didn't enjoy _e_ very much _o_ .   the time we spent in London
11 He couldn't _d_ find _r_ at once _o_ .   a hotel
12 She's learnt to ride _o_ very well _i_ .   her new bicycle
13 Do you _t_ enjoy _e_ very much _r_ ?   walking in the rain
14 My husband doesn't _g_ cook _t_ often.   dinner
15 Are we _t_ learning _c_ quickly _a_ ?   English

The Rulebox

Do not separate the

Example	5	11	3	15	7		12	1	8	10	6	14
d												

from the

2	13	9	4

B This student has left out all his adverbs because he does not know where to put them. Use a ∧ to show where each one goes. If it can go in more than one place, show all the possible positions.

Example: ∧ I start work ∧. (on Monday)

1 I don't enjoy cycling. (at all)
2 I left Beijing. (on Tuesday)
3 I'll love you. (forever)
4 Don't you get tired of studying? (sometimes)

© Macmillan Publishers Limited 1994.

Review 1

Match each phrase on the left with a phrase, *a* or *b*, on the right.

1 If you'd like some coffee, come quickly …   a) there aren't many left.
2 If you'd like some nuts, come quickly …   b) there isn't much left.

---

3 Have you seen the snow?   a) Well, if it isn't snowing, I'll go out.
4 What are you doing this evening?   b) Yes, if it weren't snowing, I'd go out.

---

5 She's never been able to get up early …   a) so she was called this morning.
6 She always gets up early …   b) so she called this morning.

---

7 Have you rung the dentist?   a) Yes, I'm going to do my teeth.
8 Do you need the toothpaste?   b) Yes, I'm going to have my teeth done.

---

9 This teacher is famous …   a) he's the man who taught Einstein.
10 This student is famous …   b) he's the man Einstein taught.

---

11 He's eaten   a) a low fat diet.
12 He's been eating   b) the whole cake.

---

13 She looks happy!   a) Yes. She's gone away.
14 Has she left?   b) Yes. She's been away.

---

15 You're always leaving early.   a) I wish you had more time.
16 You left so early …   b) I wish you'd had more time.

---

17 Something has disturbed the dogs …   a) they bark.
18 Don't wake the dogs …   b) they're barking.

---

19 Are you allergic to anything?   a) Yes, I can't eat the mushrooms.
20 Are you full?   b) Yes, I can't eat mushrooms.

Review 2

Maria is staying in Scotland. She has written a letter to her friend, Yoshiko, but she has made 17 mistakes in her English. Write the letter in your exercise book and correct the mistakes. The number of mistakes in each paragraph is written at the bottom of the page.

Paragraph number	
	Dear Yoshiko,
1	I'm sorry I haven't written to you since so long. I received your letter since six weeks but I've been very busy. As you probably know I'm in Scotland since December. I came here mainly for learning English.
2	At first it was a bit difficult because I didn't speak English well and I missed a lot of things from home. But now life is much more easier.
3	I've managed to find a work in an office in the centre of Edinburgh. It's a computer company and I'm very interesting in computers, and the people is very kind to me so I'm very lucky. It's also very good for me as I have to speak English all day long.
4	A few weeks ago I've been to a disco and met a Scottish man called Derek. He wanted that I teach him Spanish, so we the next day met again and we have fallen in love! As you can imagine, this is excellent for my English!
5	Just a moment; someone knocks at the door. I'll go and answer it.
6	That was Derek with the tickets; we will go to a concert this evening and we're leaving as soon as I will finish this letter.
7	I have moved into a larger flat and I've decided to stay here for at least a year, (it depends of Derek). Have you ever gone to Scotland? If not, why you not come and visit me before you go back to Japan? Scotland is beautiful and I would love to see you again. Please write again soon and say yes.
	With love,
	Maria

Paragraph 1 - 4 mistakes   4 - 3 mistakes   6 - 2 mistakes
               2 - 1 mistake   5 - 1 mistake   7 - 3 mistakes
               3 - 3 mistakes

© Macmillan Publishers Limited 1994.

Review 3

Maria is staying in Scotland. She has written one letter to her friend, Yoshiko, and Yoshiko has replied, so Maria has now written a second letter. She has made 18 mistakes in her English. Write the letter in your exercise book and correct the mistakes. The number of mistakes in each paragraph is written at the bottom of the page.

Paragraph number	
1	Dear Yoshiko, Thank you for your letter. I'm very happy that you will come next week. I'm meeting you at the station at 9.00, so you do not need directions to my flat. Anyway, it is dangerous around the station at night, so you don't have to go out alone. If I won't be on the platform I will see you in the station cafe.
2	I am still enjoying Scotland and Edinburgh is the beautiful city with lots of interesting places to visit. I didn't know you already visited it. How long did you stay here? I hope you have not already seen everything. Only problem is the weather; it rains a lot, nearly every day. If it doesn't rain so much I can go out more, but I have to spend a lot of time indoors, at least, at this time of year.
3	Do you remember Derek? He's the man who I wrote to you about him in my last letter. A few weeks ago he said he will take me somewhere interesting, and last week he did; on Saturday he has taken me to a castle in the mountains which built in 1370. It is having a lot of prisons underground and there's a ghost there too; of a Scottish noble who cut off his head there.
4	I enjoyed very much and, if you like, we can go there together too. Unfortunately, when we got back home, I realised I left my handbag on the bus and I had to go to the left luggage office to get it back. Luckily all my money was still in it; nobody took anything. I think people in Britain are so honest. Anyway, I'm really looking forward to seeing you. With love *Maria*

Paragraph 1 - 4 mistakes   3 - 6 mistakes
              2 - 5 mistakes   4 - 3 mistakes

Review 4

A Yesterday was a bad day for everyone. Match the pictures of what these people did yesterday with what they say today and complete their sentences.

I've read it before.   I've put odd socks on.   I've missed it.

1 _____ When I looked down at my feet I noticed _____

2 _____ As soon as I got to the harbour I saw _____

3 _____ When I got to page 50 I remembered _____

B Here are some common signs. Complete each sign by choosing the correct word or words.

1 Now that you *finished/have finished* your shopping, why not relax in our new cafeteria?

2 Faldo's. Bakers *since/for* 1890.

3 *We're going to/We'll* give you beautiful hands – no appointment necessary. Aphrodite's Parlour.

4 This door should *keep/be kept* locked at all times.

5 If you wish your neighbours *aren't/weren't* so loud, you need Senic Insulation!

6 If you haven't *slept/been sleeping*, we may be able to help you.

C This student has left out all his adverbs because he does not know where to put them. Use a ∧ to show where each one goes. If it can go in more than one place, show all possible positions.

1 Singing isn't much fun if you can't sing.   (very well)

2 I don't like driving on motorways.   (much)

3 He's coming to Vienna.   (next week)

4 I'd like to go to the Natural History Museum.   (again)

5 When I next saw her, she was married.   (after that)

6 I enjoy camping by the sea.   (really)

© Macmillan Publishers Limited 1994.

Review 5

Here are some common signs. Complete each sign by choosing the correct word or words.

Example: All breakages *should*/*must* be paid for.

1. Danger! House *being*/*been* demolished.

2. FIRE NOTICE: If the alarm *will sound*/*sounds*, go quietly to the nearest exit.

3. *If*/*Unless* your case is urgent, please come back another day.

4. **College Order:** You *mustn't*/*don't have to* walk on the lawn. The Principal.

5. **Donor Card. Carry this card with you at all times *if*/*in case* you need it.**

6. WANTED: Person *to help*/*for helping* with light housework. Tel. 62051.

7. *Not*/*No* talking please!

8. ENGLISH *spoken*/*speaks* here.

9. Smoking *no*/*not* allowed.

10. Now please wash *the*/*your* hands.

11. If you *are liking*/*like* what we do; tell your friends, if not; TELL US!

12. **Please do not feed *the elephants*/*elephants*.**

13. *Cut your hair here.*/*Have your hair cut here.* No appointment required.

14. Could you tell us as soon as possible if *are you interested*/*you are interested*?

15. Will all those *wish*/*who wish* to make an appointment please see the receptionist.

16. Evening computer courses! For all those who wish they *can*/*could* understand their personal computer.

17. Dry Cleaners. For clothes as *cleaner*/*clean* as when they were new.

18. **Mercury Travel.** We'll take you anywhere you want to go. No place *very*/*too* far for Mercury.

19. *Been*/*Gone* to lunch. Back soon.

20. Take our course and in just 10 days *you're going to speak*/*you'll be speaking* perfect French!

21. **Claim your free petrol now. Hurry, not *much*/*many* left!**

22. **Gridiron** Jack Cook's new autobiography Read it and be *shocked*/*shocking* by the truth.

23. If you *enjoyed*/*have enjoyed* her last record, you'll love *Dedication*.

24. **Not tested on animals. For people who *care*/*cares* about the environment.**

© Macmillan Publishers Limited 1994.

Answer Key

2 Adjectives with -ed and -ing 1

1 thrilled
2 amusing
3 confused
4 tiring
5 frightening
6 horrified
7 disgusted
8 shocked
9 confusing
10 surprising
11 horrifying

The hidden word is *descriptions*.

3 Adjectives with -ed and -ing 2

A
1 He feels frightened.
2 They feel exhausted.
3 They feel bored.
4 She feels excited.

B
a1 b4 c3 d2

C
a 4 very exciting.
b 1 very frightening.
c 3 very boring.

D
1a 2b 3b 4a 5b 6a

4 Adverbs of time

A
since: June, Saturday, you arrived, last weekend, he was born
for: ages, two years, nine months, quite a while, over a year

a since   b for

B
1 for   2 since   3 ago
4 for   5 ago   6 since

5 Articles 1

A
1 a   2 the   3 the   4 the

B
1 a   4 a   7 the   10 the
2 the   5 the   8 the   11 the
3 a   6 the   9 the   12 a

C
1 the   3 the   5 the
2 the   4 a   6 the

6 Articles 2

A
1b 2a 3c 4d 5e 6f

B
1 a, d, e   2 b, c, f

C
1e 2a 3c 4d 5b

7 Articles 3

1 ___
2 ___
3 the
4 the
5 ___, ___, ___
6 ___
7 the
8 the
9 ___

8 Comparing 1

A
1 Diamonds are more precious than pearls.
2 A mountain is bigger than a hill.
3 People are more intelligent than monkeys.
4 Phoning is easier than writing a letter.
5 Chocolate is sweeter than fruit.
6 A lion is more dangerous than a cat.

B
1 ... more junior.
2 ... hotter.
3 ... colder.
4 ... better.
5 ... worse.
6 ... more expensive.
7 ... cheaper.
8 ... bigger.
9 ... smaller.

9 Comparing 2

1 cheaper, longer, shorter
2 flatter, sadder, thinner, wetter
3 noisier, funnier, lazier, easier
4 more bored, more pleased, more solid, more comfortable, more fragile, more expensive, more surprising, more intelligent, more dangerous
5 better (good), worse (bad)

10 Comparing 3

A
1 ... the Empire State Building isn't as tall as the Twin Towers.
2 ... the sperm whale isn't as big as the blue whale.
3 ... the wren isn't as small as the hummingbird.
4 ... the Amazon isn't as long as the Nile.

B
1 good
2 as good as
3 younger
4 as tall as
5 older
6 more intelligent than
7 stronger
8 more confident
9 better than

11 Comparing 4

A
1 a Peter b Frank c Vince
2 a Greek b Chinese c Egyptian

B
1b 2a 3c 4d

C
1a 2d 3c 4b 5f 6e

12 Conditionals 1

A
1 If you need anything I'll get it for you.
2 If it wasn't raining I'd go swimming.
3 If I could fly I'd go to the moon.
4 If it's not the right size I'll bring it back.
5 If I was younger I'd join you.

B
1 I'd visit the Science Museum if it was/were open.
2 If the shops are open, I'll buy some new clothes.
3 I'd go to the island if it wasn't/weren't too/so far.
4 If the weather's nice, I'll go to the zoo.
5 I'd go for a sail around the harbour if there was/were enough time.

13 Conditionals 2

A
1 b, c 2 a, d

B
1 'If I got rich I'd move to Florida.'
2 'If I become president I'll build houses for everyone.'
3 'If I became president I'd build houses for everyone.'
4 'If I win a lot of money I'll give up work.'
5 'If I won a lot of money I'd give up work.'
6 'If I had a boy I'd call him Rudi.'
7 'If I have a boy I'll call him Rudi.'

C
1a 2b

14 Conjunctions 1

A
1 If   3 as long as   5 unless
2 in case   4 in case   6 when

B
1 ... it's cold/it snows
2 ... it rains/it's raining
3 ... it's open
4 ... you don't arrive very late (at night)/after 12
5 ... you buy some presents/you want to buy some presents

15 Conjunctions 2

A
1b 2a 3a 4b 5a 6b 7a 8b

B
1 If   3 as long as   5 unless
2 in case   4 when

16 Countable and uncountable 1

A
I've got a dictionary here.
We've got some practice exams next week.
We've got some food in the house.
We haven't got any practice exams next week.
We haven't got any food in the house.
We've got practice exams next week.
We've got food in the house.
We've got a lot of practice exams next week.
We've got a lot of food in the house.
There's food in the house.
There are some practice exams next week.
We haven't got much food in the house.
I haven't got many practice exams next week.

B
1 uncountable nouns
2 plural countable nouns
3 singular countable nouns

C
1 uncountable noun   6 uncountable or plural noun
2 plural noun   7 uncountable or plural noun
3 uncountable noun
4 plural noun
5 singular noun

17 Countable and uncountable 2

1 How much money would you like to change?
2 There are some people to see you, sir.
3 John hasn't got a job at the moment.
4 You find good advice in the strangest places.
5 Have you got many warm clothes with you?
6 Hurry, there isn't much time left.
7 Be careful; there is glass everywhere.
8 Here is the news.
9 Can I give some food to the animals, Mum?
10 'Ground Control, we seem to be having some trouble.'
11 He's thinking about his troubles.

18 Countable and uncountable 3

1 a   5 many   9 much   13 is
2 is   6 is   10 is   14 are
3 are   7 much   11 a
4 much   8 is   12 is

19 Countable and uncountable 4

A
1 Singular: I haven't got a, it's a
2 Plural: there are some, I haven't got many, they're
3 Uncountable: there's some, there's, I haven't got much

B
1 Singular: meal, place, group
2 Plural: people, clothes, children, feet
3 Uncountable: food, money, work, luggage, advice, information, news, traffic, furniture, fun, music, research

C
1 This is a wood.   5 These are spaces.
2 This is paper.   6 These are glasses.
3 These are papers.   7 This is glass.
4 This is space.

20 Countable and uncountable 5

A
1 problem   6 work   11 play
2 luggage   7 job   12 theatre
3 bags   8 accommodation 13 trouble
4 journey   9 hotel
5 travel   10 flat

B
1 If you're in work, you have a job.
2 If you need accommodation, there's a hotel round the corner.
3 He arrived with so much luggage that I had to carry five bags for him.
4 If you enjoy theatre, there's a good play on tomorrow night.

21 Futures 1

A
1b 2a 3a 4b 5a 6a

B
1 will/'ll   5 shall
2 is/'s going to   6 am/'m going to
3 am/'m going to   7 will/'ll
4 will/'ll

22 Futures 2

A
1b 2a 3a 4b 5b 6a

B
1 1 2 4,6 3 2 4 3,5 5 5

C
1 going to
2 will/shall
3 going to
4 will/shall
5 will/shall

23 Futures 3

1j 2f 3h 4k 5a 6i 7d 8b 9e 10c

24 Futures 4

A
1a 2b 3b 4a 5b

B

	You've just decided now.	You decided before now.	You made an arrangement with someone before now.
1	✗	✓	✓
2	✗	✓	✗
3	✗	✓	✗

C
1b 2a 3c

25 Futures 5

A
1 … he'll be reading.
2 … he'll be walking.
3 … he'll be playing football.

B
1 a … you'll be using your bike?
  b … I borrow it please?
2 a Do you think you'll be watching TV/the film at 10?
  b Well, could I watch it/the film please?
3 a Do you think you'll be seeing/ meeting Jack?
  b Well, could you give him a message, please?

C
1 forget
2 be waiting
3 post
4 be living
5 be using

26 Futures 6

A
1b 2a 3c 4d 5f 6e 7g 8h

B
1b 2b 3b 4a 5b 6b 7b 8a

C
1b 4e 5g 6a 7f 8h

27 Futures 7

1 Shall (I) carry/take …
2 … is going to erupt …
3 … 's seeing/meeting …
4 … 'll call …
5 … 'll be going …
6 … 'm going to cut …
7 … 're flying/going …
8 … 'll get …
9 Shall I put out …

28 Have something done 1

A
1 She's going to have her hair washed and cut.
2 She's going to have her shoes repaired.
3 She's going to have her eyes tested.
4 She's going to have her jacket dry-cleaned.
5 She's going to have her car serviced.

B
1 He's had the windows cleaned.
2 He's had the/some trees cut down.
3 He's had the TV repaired.
4 He's had a/the kitchen fitted.
5 He's had the carpet(s) cleaned.

29 Have something done 2

A
1b 2a 3b 4a

B
a, f

C
1 … garden done.
2 … house decorated?
3 … hair done?

30 Indirect questions

A
1 … what the hotel is like.
2 … how hot it is.
3 … what there is to do at night.
4 … if there are any good shops.
5 … how big the resort is.
6 … what the beaches are like.
7 … how high the prices are.
8 … how far away the hotel is.

B
1b 2a 3b 4a 5a 6b 7b 8a 9b 10a

31 Infinitive and gerund 1

A
1 She's brought a lawnmower to cut the grass.
2 She's brought a cat to catch the mice.
3 She's brought an axe to cut down the tree.
4 She's brought some glass to replace the broken window.
5 She's brought a caravan to live in.

B
1 … renovating houses
2 … to help (me)
3 … being alone
4 … looking for a new house
5 … moving around
6 … talking to you

32 Infinitive and gerund 2

A
1 To catch the bus.
2 To post a letter/some letters.
3 To have a bath.
4 To take (some) photos/photographs.

B
Phrases which are possible: 3, 4, 5

C
1g 2h 3e 4j 5a 6f 7d 8b 9i

33 Infinitive and gerund 3

A
1 … to see/… seeing
2 … setting up/… to set up

3 ... to be/... being
4 ... experiencing/... to experience
5 ... to earn/... earning
6 ... going/... to go
7 ... staying/ ... to stay
8 ... living/... to live

B
1 spending   5 making
2 to book   6 giving
3 to provide   7 to call
4 to deal

34 Modal verbs 1

1 should   5 should   9 can
2 can't   6 shouldn't   10 can't
3 mustn't   7 must   11 shouldn't
4 should   8 mustn't   12 can

35 Modal verbs 2

A
1c 2e 3a 4d 5f 6b

B
1 can   3 should   5 must
2 can't   4 shouldn't   6 mustn't

C
1b 2a 3c

36 Modal verbs 3

1 don't have to   5 must/have to   9 doesn't have to
2 must   6 don't have to   10 have to
3 have to   7 mustn't   11 mustn't
4 mustn't   8 have to   12 have to

37 Modal verbs 4

A
1 You mustn't get up.
2 You don't have to get up.
3 You don't have to swim.
4 You don't have to see him.
5 You mustn't swim.

B
1 You don't have to tell me ...
2 correct
3 You mustn't walk ...
4 correct
5 ... you mustn't leave lights on all over the house.
6 We don't have to play this game ...

C
1 must   2 have to

D
1 mustn't   3 Mustn't
2 don't have to   4 Don't have to

38 Passives 1

A
1 China shop   5 Factory
2 Airport   6 Car hire company
3 Hotel   7 Library
4 Restaurant

B
1 fitted   4 serviced   7 delivered
2 parked   5 served
3 prosecuted   6 heeled

C
are A: 1 3 4 5 6 7
     B: 1 2 3 4 6 7
is   A: 2
     B: 5

39 Passives 2

A
vowel change: found, left
-ght: taught, brought
-n: won, forbidden, shown
-ed: changed, allowed, accepted

B
1 are accepted   6 be taught
2 be changed   7 be shown
3 is forbidden   8 be left
4 are (not) allowed   9 were found
5 be brought   10 has been won

40 Passives 3

A
1b 2c 3d 4a

B
1b 2a 3b

C
1 were   3 are   5 was
2 will be   4 has been   6 have been

41 Passives 4

A
1 All medicines should be kept out of the reach of children.
2 All cheques should be made payable to British Gas.
3 This houseplant should be watered frequently.
4 The shelves should be fastened securely to the wall.
5 This wine should be served slightly chilled.
6 This garment should be washed separately.
7 The roses should be planted at least one metre apart.
8 The cheesecake should be allowed to thaw before serving.

B
1 This door should not be opened except in an emergency.
2 Files should not be removed from this cabinet.
3 All cups should be returned to the canteen.
4 Vehicles should not be parked in front of the entrance.

42 Past and future

Conversation 1: 1n 2i 3m 4o 5v 6t 7u
Conversation 2: 8r 9c 10f 11j 12d 13g 14k
Conversation 3: 15e 16s 17h 18p 19a

43 Past and present

A
1b 2b 3a 4a

B
1 have you been cycling   5 do you cycle
2 did you start   6 you (still) enjoy
3 taught you   7 Have you (ever) had
4 do you cycle   8 Were (you) hurt

44 Past perfect and past simple 1

Conversation 1: 1 k 2 b/d 3 i 4 h 5 e
Conversation 2: 6 f 7 b/d 8 a 9 l 10 j

45 Past perfect and past simple 2

A
1b 2a 3b 4a 5a 6b 7a 8b

B
1c 2a 3b

C
1a,c 2b,c 3b,c 4a,b 5b,c 6a,b

46 Prepositions

A
1 What on?
2 What about?
3 What with?
4 What for?
5 What in?
6 What to?
7 What of?
8 What about?
9 What for?
10 What with?

B
1 at   4 on   7 of   10 of
2 to   5 on   8 on   11 to
3 in   6 to   9 of

O	N		O	F		T	O
I	N		O	O		A	T
O	T		N	F		T	O
N	O		O	F		I	N

47 Present perfect

A
1 done   4 made   7 learnt
2 given   5 acted   8 won
3 written   6 visited

The hidden name is *Dean Watts*.

B
1 They've torn the sofa.
2 They've broken the window.
3 They've disconnected the phone/telephone.
4 They've stolen the picture.

48 Present perfect and past simple 1

A
1a 2b 3a 4b 5a 6b

B
1 started
2 was
3 trained
4 has trained/has been training
5 has played
6 is
7 has played
8 has thrown
9 is
10 have not seen

49 Present perfect and past simple 2

A
1b 2a 3a 4b 5b 6a 7b 8a

B
Present perfect: 1, 2, 4 Past simple: 3

C
1 has been   4 has joined/been
2 wrote   5 was
3 visited   6 was decimalised

50 Present perfect and past simple 3

A
1 I've been here for about nine days now.
2 I haven't been to London yet.
3 I saw a very interesting film.
4 It was about life in Scotland.
5 I'm waiting for a phone call which hasn't come yet.
All other sentences are correct.

B
1 has happened   7 met
2 have had   8 fell
3 had   9 (have) asked
4 have been   10 have been
5 have made   11 has given
6 haven't spoken

51 Present perfect and past simple 4

A
I haven't been to Brighton ...
  1 today.
  2 for a while.
  3 this winter.
  4 for a week.
  7 recently.
  8 since Tuesday.
  9 up to now.
I didn't go to Dublin ...
  1 today.
  2 for a while.
  3 this winter.
  4 for a week.
  5 yesterday.
  6 three days ago.
  7 recently.

B
1b 2a 3b 4b

C
1b 2a 3a 4b 5b 6a 7a 8b

52 Present perfect and past simple 5

Conversation 1: 1g 2e 3a 4h/i 5n 6b 7f
Conversation 2: 8c 9p 10o 11h/i 12m 13l 14k

53 Present perfect simple and continuous 1

A
1 ...'s been fishing.
  ...'s caught a crab.
2 ...'s been cooking.
  ...'s made a cake.
3 ...'s been painting.
  ...'s re-painted the ceiling.

B
1 ... I've been waiting ...   4 ...'ve been studying
2 ... I've finished ...   5 ...'s travelled ...
3 ... I've driven ...   6 ...'s been travelling

54 Present perfect simple and continuous 2

A
1a 2b 3a 4b 5b 6a 7a 8b 9b 10a 11b 12a

B
1 I've been reading this book all day.
2 I've been reading this book, but I haven't finished it yet.

3 I've read about half this book today.
4 I've read this book, but I don't remember exactly when.

C
1 present perfect continuous
2 present perfect simple
3 present perfect continuous
4 present perfect continuous
5 present perfect simple

55 Present simple and continuous 1

A
1a 2b 3a 4b 5b 6a 7b 8a

B
1 Does she speak Danish?
2 Is she speaking Danish?
3 Where do you stay in Manchester?
4 Where are you staying in Manchester?
5 What time does the plane arrive?
6 What time is the plane arriving?

56 Present simple and continuous 2

A
1 b iii   2 b i   3 a ii

B
1b 2a 3c

C
1 c ii   2 b iii   3 a i

D
1 present simple
2 present continuous
3 present continuous

57 Present simple and present continuous 3

1 are being	5 enjoys	9 tastes
2 feels	6 has	10 is feeling
3 is seeing	7 be thinking	11 thinks
4 am having	8 is enjoying	12 see

The hidden words are: *actions, states*.

58 Relative clauses 1

1 ... are the people who came for an interview.
2 ... are the people (who) I shortlisted.
3 ... is the person who didn't get back in touch.
4 ... are the people whose references I asked for.
5 ... are the people (who) I rejected.
6 ... is the woman/person who got the job.

59 Relative clauses 2

A
| 1 Jorge | 3 Gotam | 5 Steven |
| 2 Sabrina | 4 Michael | |

B
1 Frederique	4 Mrs Singh	6 Lydia
2 Min Yao	5 Mrs Roach	7 David's
3 John		

C
1a 2b 3a 4b 5a 6b

60 Relative clauses 3

1 who came to mend it
2 I put up

3 Mum and Dad took me to
4 I'd invited
5 I had asked to my party
6 I had sent/I sent
7 which makes tea
8 who told my fortune
9 you sent (me)
10 I got.

61 Relative clauses 4

A
1b 2a 3a 4a 5b

B
1a 2b 3b 4a 5b 6a

C
1b 2a 3c 4c 5c

62 Reporting 1

1 b ... it/the bench had just been painted.
2 a ... I'd missed my/the train.
3 f ... I'd run out of petrol.
4 e ... I'd been robbed.
5 c ... he'd written to me.

63 Reporting 2

A
1 ... I could do magic
2 ... I would never be able to read and write
3 ... I was going to be a doctor

B
1 ... I was 10, I promised that I was never going to/would never start smoking
2 ... I was 16, I said that I would try it just once
3 ... I was 17, I insisted that I only smoked at weekends
4 ... I was 18, I boasted that I could give up any time I liked
5 ... I was 21, I declared that I had given up
6 ... I was 25, I admitted that I couldn't give up
7 ... it was a bad idea to start in the first place

64 Reporting 3

1 ... conducted last year, 58% of people said/had said they would prefer larger cans. *or* had conducted last year, 58% of people said/had said they would prefer larger cans.
2 ... didn't always tell the truth because people often lie/lied *or* don't always tell the truth because people often lie/lied.
3 ... was absolutely necessary to go for larger cans if we wanted/want to succeed. *or* is absolutely necessary to go for larger cans if we want/wanted to succeed.
4 ... wanted larger cans, and they would pay for them.
5 ... conducted the year before 58% of people said/had said they would prefer larger cans. *or* had conducted the year before, 58% of people said/had said they would prefer larger cans.
6 ... didn't always tell the truth because people often lie/lied *or* don't always tell the truth because people often lie/lied.
7 ... was absolutely necessary to go for larger cans if they wanted to succeed.

65 Reporting 4

A
1b 2a 3a 4b 5b 6a 7c 8a 9b

B
1 ✓ 2 ✓ 3 ✗ 4 ✓ 5 ✓ 6 ✓

66 Substitution words and others

A
1 some 4 one   7 self   10 any
2 too   5 to   8 them   11 either
3 or   6 those 9 so   12 else

T	H	O	S	E	E
O	S	O	M	E	I
O	N	E	I	T	T
A	N	Y	L	O	H
E	L	S	E	F	E
T	H	E	M	O	R

B
1 has   6 did   11 doesn't
2 were   7 so   12 have
3 are   8 should 13 won't
4 had   9 do   14 not
5 will   10 can

67 Suggestions 1

A
1 ... about...   4 ... don't (we) go ...
2 ... we take ...   5 Would you ...
3 Let('s) sit ...

B
a3 b1 c2 d4 e7 f5 g6

68 Suggestions 2

A
1 Shall we go?
2 How about watching a video?
3 Why don't we go?
4 Why don't we watch a video?
5 Where shall we go?
6 Where shall we watch a video?
7 What shall we do?
8 Where would you like to go?
9 Let's go.
10 Let's watch a video.

B
Phrases which are possible: 1, 4, 7, 9

C
Phrases which are possible: 1, 3, 6, 8

D
1 Do   9 watch
2 eating   10 one
3 No   11 Shall
4 eat   12 have
5 what   13 too
6 having   14 can't
7 watching   15 not
8 that

69 Time phrases

1 tell you   5 has/'s repaired it
2 go   6 'm/am gone
3 comes in   7 come
4 have/'ve got dressed

70 Too and enough 1

A
1 Because it's too hot.
2 Because it isn't sweet enough.
3 Because they're too fat.
4 Because it's too far.
5 Because they're not old enough.

B
1 ... are too expensive to buy.
2 ... is too bright to look at.
3 ... isn't warm enough to swim in.
4 ... isn't long enough to learn ...
5 ... is too small to see.

C
1 there are too many   5 enough
2 there isn't enough   6 enough
3 there's too much   7 too many
4 there aren't enough

71 Too and enough 2

A
1a 2b 3b 4a 5a 6b

B
1 adverb   2 adjective   3 noun

C
1 water   3 strong   5 money   7 fast
2 strength 4 rich   6 speed

72 Used to

A
1d 2g 3f 4a 5b 6e

B
1 ... used to come and watch ...
2 ... used to go climbing ...
3 ... used to play ...
4 ... didn't use to play ...
5 ... didn't use to wear ...
6 ... didn't use to know ...
7 ... used to be ...
8 ... used to think ...

73 Want someone to do something

1f The customer wants the cashier to cut the string (for her).
2b The teacher wants the class to listen (to him).
3a The man wants the plumber to repair the tap.
4e The tourist wants the police officer to give her directions.
5c The tourists want the waiter to take their photograph/to take a photograph of them.
6h The girl wants the boy to play football.
7g The parachutist wants the workers to get him down.

74 Wish 1

1 ... I had more money.
2 ... I could find a job.
3 ... I wasn't/weren't sitting here by myself.
4 ... it wasn't/weren't raining.
5 ... the weather was/were better all the time.
6 ... I had/I'd got some friends here.
7 ... I could understand what people are/were saying.
8 ... David didn't/wouldn't go out all the time.
9 ... my radio was/were working.
10 ... I wasn't/weren't getting a cold.

75 Wish 2

A
1 ... I wish I had stayed

2 ... I wish we hadn't got married.
3 ... I wish we hadn't met.
4 ... now I wish she had phoned...

B
1 ... I hadn't spent all my money.
2 ... I could drive.
3 ... I didn't have to go to the dentist.
4 ... the sun was/were shining.
5 ... I had been there at the end of the party.
6 ... you had (got) more patience.
7 ... the wind wasn't/weren't blowing (so) hard.
8 ... I hadn't told him he was stupid.

76 Wish 3

A
a: 2, 5 b: 3 c: 1, 4

B
1c 2f 3e 4a 5b 6g

C
1 ... the burglar *hadn't taken* ...
2 ... you *had* told me ...
3 ... we *didn't* have to leave ...
4 ... my garden *were/was* bigger ...
5 ... I *had seen/could have seen* ...
6 I *had* known ...
7 If your house *were/was* smaller ...
8 ... my boyfriend *were/was* taller.

77 Word order

A
1 b 2 v 3 e 4 b 5 i 6 c 7 t 8 j 9 r 10 e 11 r
12 o 13 e 14 t 15 c

The hidden words are *direct object* and *verb*.

B
1 I don't enjoy cycling ∧.
2 ∧ I left Beijing ∧.
3 I'll love you ∧.
4 Don't you ∧ get tired of studying ∧?

Review 1

1b 2a 3b 4a 5a 6b 7b 8a 9a 10b 11b 12a
13b 14a 15a 16b 17b 18a 19b 20a

Review 2

Paragraph 1:
1 for so long
2 six weeks ago
3 I've been in Scotland
4 mainly to learn English

Paragraph 2:
5 life is much easier

Paragraph 3:
6 to find work/a job
7 interested in computers
8 people are

Paragraph 4:
9 I went to a disco
10 He wanted me to teach him Spanish
11 we met again the next day/the next day we met again

Paragraph 5:
12 someone is knocking

Paragraph 6:
13 we are going to a concert
14 as soon as I finish/I have finished

Paragraph 7:
15 depends on
16 Have you ever been to Scotland?
17 why don't you come

Review 3

Paragraph 1
1 ... that you are coming next week.
2 I'll meet you at the station ...
3 ... so you mustn't/shouldn't go out alone.
4 If I am not on the platform...

Paragraph 2
5 ... Edinburgh is a beautiful city ...
6 I didn't know you had already visited it.
7 The only problem is the weather ...
8/9 If it didn't rain so much I could go out more ...

Paragraph 3
10 He's the man (who) I wrote to you about in my last letter.
11 ... he said he would take me somewhere interesting ...
12 ... on Saturday he took me to a castle ...
13 ... which was built in 1370.
14 It has a lot of prisons ...
15 ... who had his head cut off there.

Paragraph 4
16 I enjoyed it very much...
17 ... I realised I had left my handbag on the bus ...
18 ... nobody had taken anything.

Review 4

A
1 b ... I'd put odd socks on.
2 c ... I'd missed it/the ferry.
3 a ... I'd read it before.

B
1 have finished   4 be kept
2 since   5 weren't
3 We'll   6 been sleeping

C
1 Singing isn't much fun if you can't sing ∧.
2 I don't ∧ like driving on motorways ∧.
3 ∧ He's coming to Vienna ∧.
4 I'd like to go ∧ to the Natural History Museum ∧.
5 When I next saw her ∧, she was married.
6 I ∧ enjoy camping by the sea.

Review 5

1 being   13 Have your hair cut here.
2 sounds   14 you are interested
3 Unless   15 who wish
4 mustn't   16 could
5 in case   17 clean
6 to help   18 too
7 No   19 Gone
8 spoken   20 you'll be speaking
9 not   21 much
10 your   22 shocked
11 like   23 enjoyed
12 the elephants   24 care

Index

a/an 5, 6, 16, 17, 18, 19, Review 3
adjectives
    adjectives with -ed and -ing 2, 3
    comparing adjectives with as ... as 10, 11, Review 5
    comparing adjectives with -er/more ... than 8, 9, 10, 11
    also see too and enough
adverbs
    adverbs and word order 77, Review 4
    adverbs of time 4, 69, Review 1
advice 34, 35, 41
ago 4
articles
    a/an 5, 6, 16, 17, 18, 19, Review 3
    the 5, 6, 7, Review 3, Review 5
    zero article 7, Review 3, Review 5
as ... as 10, 11, Review 5
as long as 14, 15
as soon as 69

been and gone 50, Review 5
before 69

can and can't 34, 35, Review 5
comparatives *see* comparing
comparing
    adjectives with as ... as 10, 11, Review 5
    adjectives with -er/more ... than 8, 9, 10, 11
conditional sentences 8, 14, 15, 30, 69, Review 1, Review 3, Review 5
    first and second conditional sentences 12, 13, Review 3
conjunctions 14, 15, 69
continuous tenses *see* simple and continuous tenses
could 25, Review 5
countable and uncountable nouns 16, 17, 18, 19, 20

defining relative clauses 58, 59, 60, 61, Review 3, Review 5
direct object 77
don't have to 34, 36, 37, Review 3, Review 5

-ed and -ing adjectives 2, 3
enough and too 70, 71
-er ... than 8, 9, 10, 11

feel like -ing 33, 67, 68
for and since 4, 50, Review 2, Review 4
future continuous 25, 26, 27, Review 5
future progressive *see* future continuous
future time
    future continuous 25, 26, 27, Review 5
    going to Review 5
    going to and will 21, 22
    going to and present continuous and will 23, 24, 27, Review 3
    in reported speech 64, 65
    present continuous with future meaning 23, 24, 27, 42, Review 2, Review 3
    shall 21, 22, 27, 42, 67, 68
    will 23, 25, 26, Review 3

gerund and infinitive 31, 32, 33, 67, 68
going to 21, 22, 23, 24, 27, Review 5
gone and been 50, Review 5

have (got) to 36, 37
have something done 28, 29, Review 5
how about -ing? 67, 68

if sentences 8, 12, 13, 14, 15, 30, 69, Review 3, Review 5
if only 74
in case 14, 15, Review 5
indirect questions 30, Review 5
indirect speech 63, 64, 65
infinitive
    infinitive and gerund 31, 32, 33, 67, 68
    infinitive of purpose 31, 32, Review 2, Review 5
    also see want someone to do something
-ing
    -ing and -ed adjectives 2, 3
    -ing and to 31, 32, 33
in order to 31, 32

let's 42, 67, 68
lot of 16

many and much 16, 17, 18, 19
mind -ing 33
modal verbs 34, 35, 36, 37
    also see can, could, don't have to, have (got) to, must, mustn't and don't have to, shall, should, will, would
more ... than 8, 9, 10, 11
much and many 16, 17, 18, 19
must 34, 35, 36, 37, Review 5
mustn't 34, 35, 36, 37, Review 3, Review 5

nouns *see* countable and uncountable

object
    direct object and word order 77
    in relative clauses 59
obligation 34, 35

passive 38, 39, 40, 41, Review 3, Review 5
past and future time 42
past and present questions 42, 43
past continuous 44, 45
past perfect
    past perfect and past simple 44, 45, Review 3, Review 4
    in reported speech 62, 64, 65
    after wish 75
past participle 38, 39, 40, 47, Review 5
past simple 42
    after wish 74, 75, 76
    in reported speech 63, 64, 65
    past simple and past perfect 44, 45, Review 3, Review 4
    past simple and present perfect 48, 49, 50, 51, 52, Review 2, Review 3, Review 4
    also see if sentences
permission 34, 35
plural and singular nouns *see* countable and uncountable nouns
prefer 33
prepositions 46, 60, 61
present and past questions 42, 43
present continuous
    present continuous and present simple 55, 56, 57, Review 2, Review 3, Review 5
    with future meaning 23, 24, 27, 42, Review 2, Review 3, Review 4
present perfect 4, 47, 69, Review 2
    present perfect and past simple 48, 49, 50, 51, 52, Review 2, Review 3. Review 4
    present perfect continuous and simple 53, 54, Review 1, Review 4
present simple 14, 15, 48, 49, 69, Review 5

in reported speech   64, 65
present simple and continuous   55, 56, 57,
    Review 2, Review 3, Review 5
also see if sentences
progressive tenses *see* simple and continuous
    tenses

questions
    indirect questions   30
    past and present questions   42, 43

rather   33, 67, 68
relative clauses (defining)   58, 59, 60, 61,
    Review 3, Review 5
reporting (indirect speech)   62, 63, 64, 65,
    Review 3

shall   21, 22, 27, 42, 67, 68
should and shouldn't   34, 35, 41, Review 3,
    Review 5
simple and continuous tenses   55, 56, 57,
    Review 2, Review 3, Review 5
since and for   4, 50, Review 2, Review 4
singular and plural nouns *see* countable and
    uncountable
some   16, 17, 18, 19
subject (in relative clauses)   59
substitution words   66
suggestions   67, 68

tenses (contrasted)
    future   Review 4
        going to and will   21, 22
        going to and present continuous
            and will   23, 24, 27, Review 3
            will and will be -ing   25, 26, 27
    past and future time   42
    past perfect and past simple   44, 45, Review 3
    present continuous and present simple   55,
        56, 57, Review 2, Review 3, Review 5
    present perfect and past simple   48, 49, 50,
        51, 52, Review 2, Review 3
    present perfect continuous and simple   53, 54
tenses *see* future continuous, future time, going
    to, past continuous, past perfect, past
    simple, present continuous, present perfect,
    present simple, shall, simple and continuous
    tenses, will
than *see* comparing
that (in relative clauses)   60, 61
the   5, 6, 7, Review 3, Review 5
time phrases   69
to   Review 5
    to and -ing   31, 32, 33
too
    too and enough   70, 71
    too and very   70, 71, Review 5

uncountable and countable nouns   16, 17, 18,
    19, 20
unless   14, 15, Review 5
until   69
used to   72

verb forms *see* tenses
very and too   70, 71, Review 5

want someone to do something   73, Review 2
when (as a conjunction)   69
which (in relative clauses)   60, 61
who (in relative clauses)   58, 59, 60, 61,
    Review 3, Review 5
whom (in relative clauses)   58, 59
whose (in relative clauses)   58, 59
why don't we ...?   67, 68
will   21, 22, 23, 24, 25, 26, 27, Review 3
    will be -ing   25, 26, 27, Review 5
    also see if sentences
wish   74, 75, 76
word order   30, 70, 71, 77, Review 2, Review 4,
    Review 5
would
    would like   28, 29, 33, 67, 68
    would love   67, 68
    would rather   33, 67, 68
    in reported speech   64, 65, Review 3
    also see if sentences